These Songs We Sing
Reflections on the Hymns We Have Loved

As a church musician and pianist, the discovery of Carla Klassen's volume of inventive hymn arrangements several years ago was like meeting a new friend with whom one feels an instant connection. In *These Songs We Sing*, Carla's written voice is as satisfying as her musical voice, creating a devotional guide for Christian discipleship as she explores why these timeless hymns resonate so deeply in our individual and collective souls.
 —Dr. Beverly Lapp
 Vice President and Academic Dean,
 Anabaptist Mennonite Biblical Seminary

Carla Klassen has taken on a self-motivated spiritual journey; one hymn per week for a year. She covers a wide spectrum in the lexicon of hymnody with astute observations, personal sharing, pertinent historical context, and storytelling. Each chapter ends with a testimony to God's grace and gentle encouragement to the reader. This study would make an ideal devotional guide.
 —Dr. Larry Nickel
 CEO of Cypress Choral Music Publishing

These Songs We Sing
Reflections on the
Hymns We Have Loved

Carla Klassen

PANDORA
PRESS

Library and Archives Canada
Cataloguing in Publication

Title: These songs we sing:
reflections on the hymns we have loved / Carla Klassen.

Names: Klassen, Carla, author.

Identifiers: Canadiana 2022041985X |
ISBN 9781926599984 (softcover)

Subjects: LCSH: Hymns—History and criticism.

Classification: LCC BV310 .K53 2022 |
DDC 264/.23—dc23

Author: Carla Klassen
Book design and editing by Maxwell Kennel
Typeset in Adobe Jenson Pro

THESE SONGS WE SING
ISBN: 978-1-926599-98-4

Copyright © 2022 Pandora Press Published by
Pandora Press
All rights reserved.

www.pandorapress.com

Acknowledgements

A lifetime of involvement in church singing is the foundation of this book. There are many congregations that have contributed to my experience with hymns, and consequently to my deep connection and love for them. I wish to thank them all, but in particular the Ottawa Mennonite Church where I have had the great pleasure of attending for the past twenty-five years. These generous people have opened their hearts through their voices with such enthusiasm that it is impossible for me to remain unmoved. So many people have encouraged me personally with frequent expressions of gratitude for my involvement and contributions. One could not ask for a better garden in which to grow. For his many years as choir director, song leader, supporter and friend, I especially wish to thank Eric Rupp.

I also wish to offer thanks to my family for providing space for lively debate and humour, and contributing to my desire to look at things carefully and with compassion. I am specifically grateful for a grandfather who collected hymns like they were gold, and a father who led so many voices to sing them.

Finally, deep gratitude goes to my husband Bryan, without whom I would never have had the nerve to send any of my work out into the world.

For my dad, who gave me music,
and my mom, who taught me
to care about people.

Table of Contents

Introduction. In the Beginning
Chapter 1. Be Thou My Vision
Chapter 2. Dona Nobis Pacem
Chapter 3. Jesus Bids Us Shine
Chapter 4. Praise To The Lord, The Almighty
Chapter 5. Now Thank We All Our God
Chapter 6. For The Beauty Of The Earth
Chapter 7. Great Is Thy Faithfulness
Chapter 8. For All The Saints
Chapter 9. There's A Wideness In God's Mercy
Chapter 10. This Little Light Of Mine
Chapter 11. Gott ist die Liebe
Chapter 12. Oh, How Shall I Receive Thee
Chapter 13. In The Bleak Midwinter
Chapter 14. Oh, How Joyfully
Chapter 15. Lo, How A Rose E'er Blooming
Chapter 16. Go Tell It On The Mountain
Chapter 17. Worship The Lord
Chapter 18. Guide Me, O Thou Great Jehovah
Chapter 19. Trust And Obey
Chapter 20. O Power of Love
Chapter 21. Just A Closer Walk With Thee
Chapter 22. When Peace, Like A River
Chapter 23. Go, My Children
Chapter 24. Take Thou My Hand, O Father
Chapter 25. Give Me Jesus

Chapter 26. What Wondrous Love Is This
Chapter 27. Ah, Holy Jesus
Chapter 28. O Sacred Head, Now Wounded
Chapter 29. Were You There?
Chapter 30. Low In The Grave He Lay
Chapter 31. And Can It Be That I Should Gain?
Chapter 32. O Perfect Love
Chapter 33. Bless'd Be The Tie That Binds
Chapter 34. When Morning Gilds The Sky
Chapter 35. Joyful, Joyful, We Adore Thee
Chapter 36. Jesus Loves Me
Chapter 37. Breathe One Me, Breath Of God
Chapter 38. I Know Not Why God's…
Chapter 39. All Creatures Of Our God & King
Chapter 40. Heilig, Heilig, Heilig
Chapter 41. Praise, My Soul, King Of Heaven
Chapter 42. In The Rifted Rock I'm Resting
Chapter 43. Be Still My Soul
Chapter 44. Come, Let Us All Unite To Sing
Chapter 45. Amazing Grace
Chapter 46. Lead Me, Lord
Chapter 47. Holy, Holy, Holy
Chapter 48. He Leadeth Me
Chapter 49. My Life Flows On
Chapter 50. Abide With Me
Chapter 51. Day Thou Gavest, Lord, Is Ended
Chapter 52. Praise God From Whom
        All Blessings Flow

Introduction

In The Beginning

A few years ago, I decided to take on a project. I'm a project person. I feel best when I have a deadline; especially if it is self-imposed. This particular project arose from a conversation that I had with my husband about a book I had recently read. The book was *Music in the Castle of Heaven* by Sir John Eliot Gardiner – a book written about J.S. Bach's life; predominantly his time spent composing choral music. It was an interesting but long read! At one point, as I was reading about Bach's first three years working in Leipzig, Germany, I mentioned to my husband Bryan that when a cantata was required for each and every Sunday, Bach simply wrote one – week after week. I marveled at the amount of work and commitment that it would take to do that. I lamented the fact that I doubted if I could even arrange a hymn a week for a year, never mind compose a whole cantata even once. Bryan said that he thought maybe I could. And so, the hymn project was born. At the time, I wondered if I should thank either Bach or Bryan, but in retrospect I see that I was inspired by one and encouraged by the other.

My plan was simple. I would collect a list of favourite hymns from family and friends and then arrange them for piano; one each week. I wasn't entirely sure of how I would present these works, but this was the starting point for what would become this book. So I put out a call. I received many responses. More than I expected. What surprised me most was what people were willing to add to their selections. Some people included stories and memories, and others provided comments and analyses. Some just gave me a title and nothing more. Others gave me lists and said they could go on and on – and some did, replying more than once! At the end of it, I was in possession of a list that represented people from 5 to 85 years old. The list also represented some who identified with the mainstream Christian Church, some who didn't, some who belonged to less mainstream congregations, a couple of atheists, and several who were a little disillusioned and even a bit angry. It was a good group to work with. I felt that it was important to look at these hymns from various points of view. I was inspired by their diversity and the possibility that music could transcend the specifics of our beliefs and provide something that we all need, wherever we may be.

As I reflected on the list of hymns that had been given to me, my little project started to take shape. I felt that I needed to share this work, despite some anxiety about doing so. Putting this creative endeavor out into the world was very personal. It left me feeling quite exposed. But, as it turns out, it was one of the most meaningful and rewarding things that I have ever done.

After some thought, I decided to arrange each hymn, and then record it on my trusty digital recorder, which was easier said than done because a single, unedited take was all that my technology and skills could achieve! I would then write a few words of reflection and post the whole thing on a blog. And so began a year of effort: a year with the constant presence of friends and relatives as I worked my way through their stories and suggestions. It was a year of anxious moments every time I clicked "post" and put my meagre offerings out into the world. It was a year of welcome and appreciated encouragement; a year of reconnections; a year of song.

I've had some time to think about this project. It's been several years since it was completed. I occasionally post a hymn on the blog, but it is not quite the same as it was when it was a weekly ritual in my life. There are, however, some things left to say. There are some thoughts, reflections, lessons, ideas, and feelings that have been percolating; things emerging from the open space between then and now.

And so, I've chosen to expand this little project, not as a scholar or researcher, but as someone who has simply come to love hymnody. My aim in this book is also to fill in some gaps that, in my mind, were left after I posted my brief comments online.

In the pages that follow I explore just a little deeper what these hymns have come to mean to me and others – to reflect on these songs we sing.

Chapter 1

Be Thou My Vision

Text: Ancient Irish, *Rob tum o bhoile, a Comdi cride*;
Translation by Mary Elizabeth Byrne, 1905
Music: Irish Melody, *Old Irish Folk Music and Songs*, 1909

How to begin a year of song? This hymn was suggested to me by a number of people as a favourite, and it seemed a good place to start. To me, this song speaks of the strength to be found in allowing whatever secures one's soul and spirit to be a guide through all we live. Faith, beliefs, and values can be both powerful and comforting if we allow them to inform the many decisions we make every day. These words speak of that power as well as the dignity, delight, shelter, wisdom, joy, and vision that come from a deep commitment to living in line with what is in our hearts.

> *Be thou my vision, O Lord of my heart;*
> *Naught be all else to me save that thou art.*
> *Thou my best thought, by day or by night,*
> *Waking or sleeping, thy presence my light.*

Be thou my wisdom, be thou my true word;
I ever with thee, and thou with me, Lord.
Thou my great Father, thy child may I be,
Thou in me dwelling, and I one with thee.

Be thou my buckler, my sword for the fight.
Be thou my dignity, thou my delight,
Thou my soul's shelter, thou my high tower.
Raise thou me heav'nward, O Pow'r of my pow'r.

Riches I heed not, nor vain empty praise;
Thou mine inheritance, now and always.
Thou and thou only, first in my heart,
High King of heaven, my treasure thou art.

High King of heaven, when vict'ry is won
May I reach heaven's joys,
O bright heav'n's Sun!
Heart of my heart, whatever befall,
Still be my vision, O ruler of all.

As I read through the words of this hymn, I was struck by how each verse had a message for me as I began this project. The messages included guidance for the year, maybe a bit of a warning, and a word or two of caution.

The song begins with the simple idea that we must consciously seek to make our deepest beliefs the very things that drive us. What a challenge! First, we must decide what these values are, and then we must follow their guidance. This sounds easy enough. But, there is much in this world that can grab and hold our attention. There is much that can capture our view and lead us in all sorts of directions. For me, the important idea in this song is that we choose what guides us, and we choose to follow that guidance. Whatever is the source of our vision, whatever provides a clear view, is ours to choose and it's ours to hold.

As I contemplated this year-long path, I wasn't entirely sure what this meant for me. I have a deeply rooted connection with the Christian Church, and more specifically with the Mennonite faith as both a belief system and a personal heritage. And yet, I have struggled with some of the specifics I have found within that broader body. What can someone who is in a constant state of questioning have to offer in matters of faith? What values and beliefs could guide this adventure? I had few answers to these questions…

The second verse of this song speaks of the wisdom that comes from one's values. In this case, the song is clearly speaking of God's wisdom, and of the process of allowing that divine wisdom to inform our decisions. The words encourage us to allow that divine wisdom to be the place in which we live. There's something sort of wonderful about that idea – the idea of dwelling within this wisdom. I could only hope to do so, and hope to express something wise through my words and music. But this was another huge challenge.

And then we arrive at the buckler verse! This hymn has a lovely tune and has some fascinating words – how often do we get to sing the word buckler? It always makes me giggle a bit when I sing these words, but when I started to think about them, I realized that I was missing the boat a bit. A buckler is a shield. It protects. The words in this verse are about safety, and about being sheltered. As I write this, I am conscious of my own insecurities in doing this project and the potential for my own beliefs to protect me from whatever it was that I feared about making myself vulnerable in this way. A solid foundation is a safe place to reside.

Finally, there are the words regarding rewards. The treasure is in the solidity of knowing what is in our hearts. Knowing. We live in a world obsessed with riches and empty praise. We know very little about what can deeply and truly satisfy our need for fulfilment. I suspect that we know very little about faith as simply faith. Maybe I'm too cynical, but it seems so often that faith is tied to rewards like heaven, salvation, health, wealth and, above all else, answers. I like the notion that what is to be gained is faith itself, grounded in values and beliefs. Maybe there are no answers. Maybe there are no rewards in the traditional sense of something that we acquire, keep, and possess. Maybe we can simply allow our lives to be guided down a path of our choosing that is filled with experiences, challenges, questions, joys, pain and treasures, all illuminated by the brightness of Heaven's Sun. Maybe that's what gives us vision and allows us to see.

So I began my year of song in this way, by desiring some vision, but not quite knowing what it was. I was full of anxiety and questions; excited and eager. It was a good place to be and to begin. It led me to people and places I would not have found otherwise. It is my heart of hearts.

Chapter 2

Dona Nobis Pacem

Text: Traditional
Music: Anonymous

I suppose that I should have started out by defining what a hymn is. The word hymn comes from the Greek word *hymnos*, which means a song of praise. This is a fairly common definition, but many also add that a hymn is a song of joy, thanksgiving, adoration, and prayer. While most of us probably associate hymns with the Christian church, it would be difficult for one religious group to claim them entirely. The ancient Egyptians had hymns, as did the ancient Greeks (the Homeric Hymns), the Hindu tradition (the Vedas) and of course, we can't forget the Psalms of the Jewish tradition. I'm sure there are many others, past and present. There is something quite basic about using words and music to express our deepest emotions.

This understanding of the diversity and history of hymnody brings us to *Dona Nobis Pacem*. I suppose that it isn't usually thought of as a hymn, but it is well known and sung by people with all sorts of beliefs. I've heard it everywhere from churches and schools, to rallies and protests. The words simply mean: *grant us peace*. When I chose to arrange this hymn, it was around September 21st, which is the United Nations International Day of Peace. At the time, it felt that we were routinely inundated with news of horror, war, unrest, poverty, and injustice. Sometimes the news reports seemed very distant, and sometimes they seemed very close. Sometimes news events were massive and overwhelming, while at other times they seemed sudden or longstanding, and still other news stories felt personal or unknown. I don't think that things have changed much since then. We are conscious of terrorism, racial unrest and injustice, the pain and frustrations of many marginalized groups, the plight of the homeless and those desperately seeking new homes, gender inequality, and violence against women.

I sometimes wonder if, in our endless pursuit of peace, we really understand what exactly peace is. As I wrote this, there was a social media maelstrom surrounding the idea of white privilege and its impact upon racism – a troubling reality that has been challenged and debated in the ensuing years. The stories of lost Indigenous children in Canada and elsewhere has recently become very real for many people, and yet the backlash against the idea that privilege is part of the problem remains baffling. If my privilege stands on the back of your struggle, then where can peace be found? We are at a loss as to how to achieve peace because it means something different depending on where you are standing. Some of us need to relinquish a bit of what we have, others need to receive a little, or a lot, more. This is a challenging reality for all.

So I offer a hymn of prayer. It is a song sung in many places, by many differing voices, when we are at a loss as to how to achieve peace. There are times when it is difficult to know what else to do but cry these very familiar words:

Dona Nobis Pacem.
Dona Nobis Pacem.
Dona Nobis Pacem.

Chapter 3

Jesus Bids Us Shine

Text: Susan Warner, 1863
Music: Edwin O. Excell, 1868

Three weeks into my yearlong project I found myself deviating from the original list of hymns provided to me by my friends and family. Shortly before I decided to add this one to my list, I had been looking for something that reflected the theme of 'light' that was planned for an upcoming church service. I needed to play a prelude for that service and I wanted something new and textually relevant. After flipping through a couple of hymnbooks, this little gem popped up. It is an old Sunday school song that I hadn't thought of in years – maybe not since I was a child. Both the words and the tune are quite simple.

> *Jesus bids us shine,*
> *With a pure, clear light,*
> *Like a little candle,*
> *Burning in the night.*
> *In this world of darkness,*
> *We must shine—*
> *You in your small corner,*
> *And I in mine.*

This is an easy concept for children to grasp, but perhaps it is a more difficult one for adults who are laden with the implications of language and ideas that can be understood differently depending on one's experience of the world. At the time I began to write about it, I chose to accept a simple interpretation of its words. While all is not right with the world, we do have the opportunity to bring to it something pure and clear.

Looking back on this selection, I find myself reflecting on whether a deeper understanding of these words is necessary. What does it really mean to shine in our world? Is it about being good or doing what is right? Who decides what is good and right? In some ways we live in complicated times. What I believe is sometimes in conflict with what you believe; and many people want to encourage and celebrate diversity. And, I think we should. To me the complexity of humanity is a beautiful thing. How we each shine will be unique. What we choose to shine upon will be different. Whose paths we brighten will vary.

But there are foundations that can inform this diversity and can make it constructive rather than destructive. Thinking about these simple words and the idea that we can choose to brighten our world in many ways, reminded me of the words of Martin Luther King. He said, "Hatred paralyzes life; love releases it. Hatred confuses life; love harmonizes it. Hatred darkens life; love illuminates it."[1] It is much easier to determine what is good and just if one looks through the illuminating lens of love; love as a deeply humble concept; and love as a gift, not a reward. Love does not require us to all be the same. It requires us to see beyond ourselves, all the while keeping our eyes on ourselves and our internal and external behaviour, with strength enough to shine. Simple, maybe. Challenging, definitely.

This idea of illuminating what is good and right is complicated by our diversity. I have recently listened to the words of many people who argue that legality is the standard by which we must make our decisions. The idea being that there is some Biblical imperative for us to honour our leaders. I'm unsure. Some laws are simply unjust. Perhaps a humble children's song can guide us towards understanding that a pure, clear light will reveal our flaws as a society. Perhaps this song that we sing can show us that the candle burning through the night lights a path through those flaws toward something better – and, perhaps, it reflects a commitment to the endless struggle of those choosing to show a way that takes us beyond where we are; beyond our failings.

I continue to ponder this simple child's song. Its words require me to consider who I am, where I am

---

[1] Martin Luther King, Jr. *Strength to Love* (Minneapolis, Minnesota: Fortress Press, 1981), 122.

from, and how I have been privileged. My desire is that from my small corner, I will see you in yours. Perhaps if we shine well enough, we will see each other. Perhaps, in our light, we can discover many wondrously dark corners and find better ways to traverse this world, and as a reward, experience an immense beauty illuminated by us all.

Chapter 4

Praise To The Lord, The Almighty

Text: Joachim Neander, 1680
Translation by Catherine Winkworth, 1863
Music: *Erneuerten Gesangbuch*, 1665

It was autumn when I visited this hymn. I love the autumn. The crisp weather, the sunshine through the changing leaves, the magnificent colours I am fortunate to see in the eastern Ontario landscape where I live. It is a time when many of my favourite activities get started, and yet we also celebrate the end of summer, the harvest, and in doing so we are thankful. As I was anticipating Thanksgiving the following week, this hymn of praise seemed appropriate. It was suggested to me by friends who shared that it had been sung at their wedding. They both expressed how meaningful it was before this event, and how much more it became after.

> *Praise to the Lord, the Almighty,*
> *the King of creation!*
> *O my soul, praise Him,*
> *for He is thy health and salvation!*
> *All ye who hear,*
> *now to God's temple draw near;*
> *Praise Him in glad adoration.*

Praise to the Lord,
who over all things so wondrously reigneth,
Shelters thee under His wings, yea,
so gently sustaineth!
Hast thou not seen
how thy heart's wishes have been
Granted in what He ordaineth?

Praise to the Lord,
who doth prosper thy work and defend thee;
Surely His goodness and mercy here
daily attend thee.
Ponder anew what the Almighty can do,
As with His love He befriends thee.

Praise to the Lord,
O let all that is in me adore Him!
All that hath life and breath,
come now with praises before Him.
Let the "Amen" sound from His people again,
Gladly forever adore Him.

This is a song of adoration. The words were originally written by Joachim Neander in German in 1680, and then translated into English in 1863 by Catherine Winkworth. I am often struck by how some of these hymns span hundreds of years and can still provide meaning and inspiration to us. My favourite bits are in the second and last verses.

Verse two speaks of how God *"shelters thee under his wings, yea, so gently sustaineth."* What an image. I can understand why someone would choose this song to mark the beginning of a marriage. It is both celebratory and filled with the promise of care.

The final verse has a statement that chokes me up every time I find myself singing it with others:

Let the "amen" sound from God's people again.

There is something very powerful about voices joining together in an "amen" – something sort of primal. The word is a declaration of affirmation. It comes up in Greek, Hebrew, Arabic, and English – with variations in many other languages and is used in all sorts of religious practices. It kind of means that we agree. Maybe it's a bit naive to think we actually agree on much – and as we look around the world it seems that we really, really don't agree on even the most basic ideas and values. But there is something spirit-building about being in a space with people and choosing to say "amen" despite our differences. This means choosing to look for ways to work together while seeking something better; encouraging positive change, acceptance, peace and kindness. It's idealistic I know, but when I sing this hymn it reminds me of that possibility on a very basic emotional level.

In whatever way that you choose to say amen, and with whatever group you choose to do so, I hope that this can be a reminder of how important it is to find a community with which to share your celebrations, your adorations, and your songs. And when we, in our own small communities, choose to really see other communities, perhaps we grow. We sing our amens in many ways and for many reasons, but perhaps there is space for us all. Let us make space to recognize how our various communities are good and valuable; space to celebrate the multitude of ways that we lift each other up and find beauty and divinity as we walk this earth. May we do so gladly and in adoration.

Amen.

Chapter 5

Now Thank We All Our God – *Nun danket alle Gott*

Text: Martin Rinckart, *Jesu Hertz-Büchlein*, 1636
Translation by Catherine Winkworth, 1858
Music: Johann Crüger, *Praxis Pietatis Melica*, 1647

Thanksgiving. It's a time to be thankful, to celebrate the harvest, to share with family and friends. A celebration of thanks is done in many, if not all, cultures at different times of the year. It is one of the few festivals that can be claimed by pretty much all of the religious groups I can think of – it is no one's exclusive ritual or creation. What strikes me about the act of giving thanks is that, despite our tendency to do so by making lists of what we have, we often need to do it much more when we have very little, be it material, physical, or spiritual. There is something strangely healing about giving thanks. It seems to provide a path to peace in turbulent times and somehow allows for a breath in the midst of struggle.

This hymn was suggested by several people, but none in English! Not surprising, as it is an old German hymn written by Martin Rinckart in the mid 1630s. Rinckart was a Lutheran minister in

Saxony who sheltered victims of disease and famine at the beginning of the Thirty Years' War. It is said that around the time he wrote this, as the only surviving minister in his city, he was performing up to fifty funerals a day. It is quite beyond me to imagine how these words could have sprung out of that kind of horror, but here again I am struck by the mystery of human strength and the power of faith.

> *Now thank we all our God,*
> *with heart and hands and voices,*
> *Who wondrous things has done,*
> *in whom this world rejoices;*
> *Who from our mothers' arms*
> *has blessed us on our way*
> *With countless gifts of love,*
> *and still is ours today.*
> *O may this bounteous God*
> *through all our life be near us,*
> *With ever joyful hearts*
> *and blessed peace to cheer us;*
> *And keep us in His grace,*
> *and guide us when perplexed;*
> *And free us from all ills,*
> *in this world and the next!*

The tune is attributed to Johann Crüger and was used by J. S. Bach in a number of his cantatas. It is a beautiful melody with very familiar harmonies thanks to Mendelssohn, and I must admit that I had some personal trepidation making changes as I arranged it for piano! However, it was also inspiring to think that for almost 400 years, this hymn has provided a reminder to be thankful even when we are perplexed, and to be cheered even when in the midst of this world's ills. It is this shared experience, this kind of history, that I am most excited by when looking at these hymns. It is both astounding and reassuring that as our world changes – for good, for bad – we can face our circumstances with some of the same tools our ancestors used. We can share their words and music by singing together across time all while being thankful for that which is beyond the immediate; a view above our own chaos.

Thankfulness is a bit of a mystery. It can serve to remind us of all we have. It can focus us on potential and opportunity. It can open our eyes to the smallest thing that carries us through whatever storm we find ourselves weathering. When I originally wrote this, I wasn't quite sure if I should include in this Thanksgiving entry a list of what I'm thankful for. This is because when I read the words of this hymn, I feel a sense of thankfulness much deeper than something that can be listed. But I am thankful for those who have come before, for those who I know now, and for those yet to experience this beautiful flawed world.

Chapter 6

For The Beauty Of The Earth

Text: Folliott S. Pierpoint, *Lyra Eucharistica*, 1864
Music: Conrad Kocher, *Stimmen aus dem Reiche Gottes*, 1838

According to my original records, the day that I wrote about this hymn was gloomy. The weather was unusually warm for October, but too muggy for my notion of a traditional crisp, autumn day. And yet, there can be such beauty in the contrast of the colours of the changing leaves against the dark, cloudy sky. Somehow, this contrast allows us to see the range of oranges and yellows in a different way than on a sunny day.

> *For the beauty of the earth,*
> *for the glory of the skies...*

The story goes, that this hymn was written by Folliott Pierpoint as he went for a stroll on a spring day in 1864. He was reportedly inspired by the beauty of the English countryside, and having experienced its beauty myself, I can understand the source of his inspiration. What he observed gave rise to a poetic text filled with gratitude, praise, and beautiful imagery.

For the beauty of each hour,
of the day and of the night,
Hill and vale, and tree and flower,
sun and moon, and stars of light...

Pierpoint speaks so beautifully of what he sees in nature, but he doesn't stop there. He includes a verse with the simple thought of finding joy in our family and friends.

For the joy of human love,
brother, sister, parent, child,
Friends on earth and friends above,
for all gentle thoughts and mild...

Such lovely sentiments. Deep within them, I see a reminder to find beauty in the whole range of what we see and experience in both the natural world and in our relationships. Day and night; hill and vale; those who are with us and those already gone. Beauty exists – on a gloomy or a sun filled day.

This our hymn of grateful praise.

We live at a time when the concept of beauty has been tarnished beyond recognition. Conversations about beauty focus on the superficial, the material, the fleeting. What is beautiful today is not tomorrow. We seek instant beauty rather than that which takes time, effort, challenge, skill, and commitment to achieve. We are wowed by the artificial, impressed by what we have manipulated to our tastes, and we forget to look closely at what is real, authentic, and true. We judge based on preference rather than on intrinsic value and endurance. We reject that which has stood the test of time in favour of what is new and exciting.

Beauty can exist in all of these extremes, but I often wonder if our preoccupation with change and trends has given rise to an inability to really appreciate the value of deep beauty; of beauty that can make our souls soar; of beauty that can inspire us to be better; of beauty that is simple and profound enough to bind us together and carry the weights we must carry. This is the beauty of human love; the beauty of the earth; the beauty of each hour. These are slow moving beauties – fully available to all if we are willing to stop and look, and to give and receive.

Chapter 7

Great Is Thy Faithfulness

Text: Thomas O. Chisholm, *Songs of Salvation*, 1923
Music: William Runyan, *Songs of Salvation*, 1923

We have arrived at one of the most frequently requested hymns on my list for my year of songs. I don't suppose that the reason for this is a great mystery – it is a hymn so familiar, with words that bring real comfort and assurance. Written in 1923, it tells of God's faithfulness throughout a lifetime. These are words that speak to the magnitude of the Divine. I love that it unapologetically requires me to consider something greater than myself.

> *Summer and winter and springtime and harvest,*
> *Sun, moon, and stars in their courses above;*
> *Join with all nature in manifold witness,*
> *To Thy great faithfulness, mercy and love.*

I received quite a few stories and comments from those suggesting this hymn as a favourite. A number of people mentioned that this had been sung at a funeral for someone close to them. Some shared that certain words brought tears. Some felt that it provided a glimpse into the character of God. The song definitely carries with it meaning and memories that are evoked whenever it is sung or heard. This is a powerful thing to be found in familiar texts and music. It is such a miracle of creativity to achieve this impact, and this is a reason why I believe we must protect our sacred arts and see them for the treasures they are.

It happened to be Mennonite Heritage Sunday when I first sat down to consider this hymn, and I thought it would be appropriate to ponder something that reminded me of where I came from. It's something that brings up memories of lives lived under the canopy of this great faithfulness. While it is not a Mennonite hymn as such, this is one of my father's favourites, and one he also put on my list. Now, I should share that I come from a long line of hymn lovers. Both my father and his father before him were musicians who actively participated in church music and were involved in compiling hymns for several new hymnals. In fact, my grandfather was also a collector of hymnals – probably acquiring in the neighbourhood of six hundred! My husband's fondest memory of him is being shown his tiny closet of a computer room where, for the last five years of his life, he entered more than 13,000 song titles and melodies into a data base as a record of all these hymns of faith that he obviously cared for deeply. Music is a gift that I was given by those who came before me. It has been, and will always be, my inheritance.

All I have needed Thy hand hath provided.

As I worked on this hymn, I thought about this gift of music. It came to me through the family I was born into, through the church I was raised in. These hymns may mean something different to me than they did to my grandfather, but they provide a solid foundation to stand on. These songs were valued, deeply. The music, words, assurance, and comfort reflect a memory, a heritage.

Strength for today,
and bright hope for tomorrow,
Blessings all mine, with ten thousand beside.

Chapter 8

For All The Saints

Text: William Walsham How, *Hymns for Saints' Days and Other Hymns*, 1864
Music: Ralph Vaughan Williams, *The English Hymnal*, 1906

All Saints' Day was an obvious point in the liturgical calendar to spend some time with this hymn, one that had been suggested to me by a few people who claimed it as a favourite. When I began to consider what this festival was about, it occurred to me that I couldn't really recall hearing much about All Saints' Day when I was growing up, and I must admit to not knowing much about it other than often singing this hymn at church. After a bit of reading, I came to understand that it was a day set aside to honour Saints, known and unknown.

Depending on one's tradition, culture, or religious affiliations, this can mean those beatified as Saints or those departed who have not yet reached heaven. It can simply be all who are currently part of the church or community, or deceased members of a congregation. The roots of this festival are ancient, and variations of it are observed in many cultures. In ancient Gaelic and Celtic traditions, it was a time when dead souls were thought to revisit their homes – and a warm welcome would bring blessings. The Mexican Day of the Dead celebration that has its roots in an Aztec festival is a national holiday dedicated to prayer and remembrance of family members that have died.

It seems to be a time to consider the spiritual connections between those living and those already gone and, whatever you believe, there is something comforting in the thought that we are still connected to our loved ones after they die. It is a way of coping with grief and loss. It is a way to understand the greatest mystery of life. It is a way to find both peace and hope.

I will admit to having some difficulty with the words of this hymn. And there are many. Although most hymnals don't include them all, I found a record of at least eleven verses. There are many expressions of conquering, winning a fight, and triumphant uprising. I understand that these images are meaningful to some, but I find them challenging. I have trouble with militaristic God imagery, and it comes up often in hymns. I suppose that I lean towards a more peaceful understanding of the Divine, and as I've discovered in many hymn texts, that can be found here as well. There is a verse that speaks of community, fellowship, and inspiration to those still living.

O blest communion, fellowship divine!
We feebly struggle, they in glory shine;
All are one in Thee, for all are Thine.
Alleluia, Alleluia!

What a lovely thought. To think of those who are gone in this way – sort of beaming from afar to show us a way. Maybe this song provides an historical perspective and experiential wisdom to help us see and understand the realities of our present. It provides a beautiful reason to examine the lives of those who have gone before; those who have lived this life and passed through its challenges; those who have crossed to another side. There is much to be learned in this illumination – good and bad. Our path is lit by both successes and failures, and different standards for what makes for a success and failure. But these successes and failures teach us about what has come before that we should emulate, and what has come before that we must never repeat.

In contemplating all the many saints who I have known, heard of, and imagined, I also find the very first line of the first verse quite moving.

For all the saints, who from their labors rest...

Again, regardless of what you believe, there is something reassuring about the rest that can be found in death. Life is a labour. It is an act of constantly doing something, and whether we sail through with ease or struggle endlessly, it is about motion and activity. The rest found in death is beyond my understanding, but I imagine it to be a kind of peace that encircles one fully. I suppose death is not something that we're very good at understanding or embracing, but it is something we all share. Celebrating those who have already walked this road is a sacred act, one filled with sadness, joy, fear, memory, anguish, and calm.

The golden evening brightens in the west;
Soon, soon to faithful servants cometh rest;
Sweet is the calm of paradise the blessed.
Alleluia, Alleluia!

Chapter 9

There's A Wideness In God's Mercy

Text: Frederick William Faber, *Oratory Hymns*, 1862
Music: Lizzie Tourjée, *Hymnal of the Methodist Church with Tunes*, 1877

Back in 2014, several weeks before I wrote about this hymn, I found myself with a free afternoon because most of my piano students had cancelled their lessons. This was not something that happens very often, and it wasn't a gift of free time. There had been a shooting at Canada's War Memorial in Ottawa and children were stuck in locked down schools or with no bus service to get to my home studio. One young boy did come for his lesson that evening and asked for the door to be locked, just in case the bad guy with the gun was still around. It was a really sad day.

I spent that time working on this hymn, and I posted my thoughts along with the arrangement on Remembrance Day of that year.

In the Mennonite Church, as pacifists who desire justice and peace, we recognize the Sunday closest to Remembrance Day as Peace Sunday. I suspect that regardless of religious affiliations, we all abhor violence and I hope we all long for peace. Our definitions and approaches to this end may vary, but few prefer violence as a way of life. Events like this shooting make me wonder if peace will ever be achieved. So much has happened in the years since this event that I find myself discouraged. However, I am also reminded that I am incredibly fortunate to live in a place where this single act is a rarity. There are many places in the world – some very close, some very far – where this would be a common occurrence. The location of the shooting at our war memorial reminds me of the many wars throughout history and those that rage now. So many complicated thoughts emerge; difficult emotions, reactions, and prayers.

A friend of mine mentioned that this was a favourite and meaningful hymn. In thinking about war, violence, and peace, I was struck by these words.

> *There's a wideness in God's mercy,*
> *Like the wideness of the sea;*
> *There's a kindness in His justice,*
> *Which is more than liberty.*

We certainly all need mercy. To be recipients of mercy that is as wide as the sea is almost too great a gift to contemplate. Are we able to be that compassionate in return? We all have a role in shaping the world we live in. When we demand justice are we capable of doing it in kindness? I'm not sure I often think in those terms. I am also impressed by the idea that justice isn't merely about liberty. We hear a lot about fighting for freedom and ensuring that all are free. These are admirable sentiments, but justice is about more than that. Justice is complicated when freedom for one means chains for another.

> *But we make God's love too narrow*
> *By false limits of our own;*
> *And we magnify its strictness*
> *With a zeal God will not own.*

As in many hymn texts, the writer of these words directs us to the immensity of God. It is our humanness that makes God small and tries to claim definitions of justice and mercy by treating them like rules and regulations. The impact of this possessive desire on our world has been great. Many acts of violence and discrimination have been done in the name of a small, humanly constructed God. When we consider peace and justice, it is my hope that we do so from the perspective of the wideness of God's mercy and love, not the limits of our own understanding or our greed and our personal comfort, our desire to be right, and our frequent belief that we are right, in absolute terms. The mercy is for all of us because there is none among us who doesn't require its healing power for what we've done, what we haven't done, what we've experienced, and what we've been spared from.

Chapter 10

This Little Light Of Mine

Text: Unknown, possibly Harry Dixon Loes, 1920
Music: Unknown, possibly Harry Dixon Loes, 1920

I often hear good stories from my students during their lessons, and during the week I first wrote about this song they happened to be about their various experiences with the minute of silence on Remembrance Day. Most of their reflections were pretty funny, involving things that, shall we say, broke the silence. While the stories were accompanied by giggles, they all seemed to know that this moment of reflection was important and that disturbing it, while funny, wasn't exactly how things should have gone. These stories and reactions are one of the many reasons that I like working with children. They see the world with a clarity that is both entertaining and humbling. The songs that have been written for children often do the same.

This song was suggested to me by a friend whose young son was rocking out to it at the time when I asked for hymn suggestions. She also forwarded me a video of the Bruce Springsteen version he was listening to. I'm pretty sure I didn't adequately rock out with my version, but working on this was a good reminder of how some songs with such sheer simplicity can catch the attention of a wide range of us – the young, the old, the rockers, and the piano players. Music is funny that way. No matter how we try to define, categorise, analyse, and understand it, sometimes we just like a tune. And sometimes the words make us think beyond what they were intended for.

This one has an interesting story. There is a sense that it is an old African American Spiritual song, and it does indeed have ties with the Civil Rights Movement in the 1950s and 1960s, but it was originally written as a children's gospel song. In the late 1930s, John Lomax, a musicologist and folklorist, included it in a collection of American folk songs. Used by activist Zilphia Horton (who also helped transform "We Shall Overcome" into a civil rights anthem) as one of the many hymns that were claimed as songs to forward the movement, it has long been sung by activists to represent the idea of shining brightly for what is right. For refusing to diminish until the task is complete.

This little light of mine, I'm gonna let it shine.
Let it shine, let it shine, let it shine.

There are several versions of this song, a few variations on the tune and some additional verses. Most are very simple. The version I remember as a child, had a verse that provided a list of daily gifts; ideas to help us through each day.

> *Monday gave me the gift of love,*
> *Tuesday peace came from above,*
> *Wednesday told me to have more faith,*
> *Thursday gave me a little more grace,*
> *Friday told me to watch and pray,*
> *Saturday told me just what to say,*
> *Sunday gave me the power divine*
> *just to let my little light shine.*

Challenges abound in our lives. Big ones – like working for the ideals of peace and justice. Small ones – like honouring a silence when we are trying not to giggle! I'm thankful for the many children I meet each week who are so vibrant, who provide both entertainment and insight in many, many ways. They remind me that even the smallest light can brighten our sometimes gloomy world. They often shine despite themselves. But I find the daily instructions in these words interesting. We start in love and hopefully have peaceful beginnings. And yet, by Wednesday we need faith, and Thursday something has been done that requires grace. By Friday all we can do is watch and pray until wisdom is revealed on Saturday, and we emerge powerful to shine for what we believe. The sequence of our lives – maybe it happens over and over – isn't instant, nor is it effortless. But we can choose to shine.

Perhaps we cannot shine every day, but we can do so often and with whatever strength our flame has to offer. This is because a little light is still a light. As is a light that needs grace or is filled with divine power. I wish to be Sunday's light for someone stuck on Friday, and I hope to receive Tuesday's light when at the bottom of Wednesday. These flames we carry are varied and exchangeable. So, let your light shine when you can, and then bask in the warmth of someone else's when yours is low.

Chapter 11

Gott ist die Liebe

Text: August Rische, 1852
Music: Thüringer Melody

The end of the liturgical calendar is celebrated with the final feast of the Christian year before things start over again with Advent. Sometimes called "Christ the King" Sunday, it is meant to be a reminder of Christ's power and the related gifts given by God. This festival was only established in 1925 by the Roman Catholic Church and was, at the time, meant to challenge the secularization of society. Well, I can't say I'm particularly concerned with or interested in this sort of focus, but I do kind of like the idea of saying goodnight to one year, reflecting on what's occurred, and then moving into the new year with a spirit of peace and gratitude.

So, I present a lullaby.

It was suggested by a friend's father who was, at the time, in his eighties. He shared that he had very clear and fond memories of his grandmother singing this to him when he was a small boy. It is another hymn I hadn't thought of in a while, and this story triggered my own memories of my mother singing this to me. Now, I am not the most reliable for memory recollection, so I consulted with my brother and sister and both confirmed that this was indeed our lullaby. My brother thought that our maternal grandmother sang it as well.

The hymn is said to be a traditional Moravian song that first shows up in print in a German songbook around 1693 (despite being attributed as a Thüringer folk song from around 1840). So it is old and has, based on what I've been told, been sung to children for at least eighty years — but very likely many, many more.

Gott is die Liebe, lässt mich erlösen;
Got ist die Liebe, er liebt auch mich.
Drum sag' ich noch einmal: Gott is die Liebe.
Gott ist die Liebe, er liebt auch mich.

I can't even hear this one in English, but the gist of it is that God is love and loves even me. Another simple, comforting sentiment. This can mean many things and probably varies for whomever is interpreting it, but for me it speaks of our intrinsic value. Something as great as a divine being loving me is a powerful source of strength. However, we see the details of the Divine, this kind of recognition and care requires us to be more than we sometimes feel or think we can be. What a lovely thing to sing to a child.

When we end one year and think of starting the next, my hope is that this reminder serves to encourage us to learn from the past and prepare for the future with the knowledge of this almighty, loving support. We are worth so much in the grand scheme of the universe. And it is not lost on me that my own value also implies the value of everyone around me. Understanding one's own worth opens up an immense responsibility both to the self and to those we share the planet with. The concept that God loves me is meaningless if others are not also loved. Perhaps it is the power of this truth that could save our chaotic and selfish world. Surely we are called to value what the Divine has deemed worthy, be they far or near.

Chapter 12

Oh, How Shall I Receive Thee

Text: Paul Gerhardt, *Praxis Pietatis Melica*, 1653
Music: Melchoir Teschner, 1613

With this hymn, we enter the Advent season; the beginning of the church year. Each week leading up to Christmas has traditionally had an associated theme – hope, peace, joy and love. The first Sunday, in my tradition, usually focusses on the idea of hope. This is a time of preparation; of expectation for what is to come.

> *Oh, how shall I receive thee,*
> *how meet thee on thy way?*

I think that many of us are weary of the excesses associated with Christmas in our culture. Weary of the seemingly never ending season of shopping, music, and decoration that precedes this annual event. I find myself having quite mixed feelings about both Christmas and Advent. On the one hand, I grow tired of hearing Jingle Bells over and over and over. On the other, there is something kind of magical about a six or seven-year-old being so excited by the ability to perform this simple song. Maybe there is a lesson there for me. There is hope to be found in the innocent excitement that children exhibit at this time of year, and a reminder of anticipation in its joyful potential.

Hope can be found in such small things, especially when we are children. But as we grow, experience, and learn of all that is difficult in our world, it becomes more challenging. Yet, the Advent season can be a time to consider that there is something greater than our decorations and festivities; something greater that can carry us through when we need hope most.

Oh, love beyond all telling,
that led thee to embrace,
In love, all love's excelling,
our lost and troubled race.

Clearly this hymn is speaking of the impending arrival of Jesus. His birth represents the ultimate gift given by God. There is hope for all of us in this concept of love being a driving force to carry us through whatever troubles we encounter. It is not limited to those who believe in the specifics of the Christian story. The examples of God's love, the gift given as a selfless act, and the good will associated with it, are powerful. We are all able to consider how this can influence our festive spirits. Will our actions over the next four weeks bring loving hope to those around us? Do the gifts we share, the music we sing, the gatherings we attend, bring hope?

When I prepare for Christmas and find myself listening to yet another version of Jingle Bells, I desire to do so in the spirit of attempting to be a beacon of hope. This is probably fairly difficult, but I think that a commitment to this perspective can temper the chaos and glitter of the season we find swirling around us. Maybe, for someone with little to celebrate, it can offer some reassurance. The hope we need is best realised when shared, for many people find this time of year to be deeply lonely and deeply sad, and I wonder if there is any point to it if we miss the opportunities to encourage and carry those who are unable to see the joy that the future holds.

Thou comest Lord, with gladness,
in mercy and good will,
To bring an end to sadness
and bid our fears be still.

Chapter 13

In The Bleak Midwinter

Text: Christina Rosetti, ca. 1872
Music: Gustav Theodor Holst, 1906

I love this carol, and it seems like I'm not the only one. In 2008, the Harold Darke setting (the choral version we all know) from 1911 was honoured as the best Christmas carol in a poll of choirmasters and choral experts. I have to say, I was really pleased to receive it on my list for my year of hymns! For those who know me, I'm sure it will come as no surprise that I lean towards the melancholy, at least musically, and this one definitely falls into that category.

The words are based on a poem written by Christina Rosetti. What words they are! – so stunning. Such a picture of a peaceful winter's night. So bleak and beautiful all at the same time.

> *In the bleak mid-winter,*
> *Frosty wind made moan,*
> *Earth stood hard as iron, water like a stone;*
> *Snow had fallen, snow on snow, Snow on snow,*
> *In the bleak mid-winter, Long ago.*

Now, I will admit that there are probably some problems with the whole description of the birth of Jesus found here. I do understand that Bethlehem isn't exactly located in the snow covered, British countryside, and that midwinter may be an arbitrary date selected to coincide with winter festivals of old. I can live with this. The notion of the bleak midwinter being a metaphor for how hard hearted and cold we and our world can be, seems fitting. Maybe finding warmth in the potential arising from the birth of this child is a good way to read this one.

The theme of peace is usually recognised on the second Sunday of Advent. I find this carol very peaceful. I find a cold, dark, and clear winter night peaceful. And yet, I am reminded regularly that we do not live in a peaceful world. It is easy to forget at this time of year that buried beneath the glitter of the season lies a small idea that provides an opportunity to encourage the peace most of us are looking for. For me, the very last verse sums this up. It speaks about how we are equipped to give the gift of ourselves; our hearts. We are good enough for this Son of God. Surely that speaks to how much we have to offer this world.

> *What can I give Him, Poor as I am?*
> *If I were a shepherd I would bring a lamb;*
> *If I were a wise man I would do my part;*
> *Yet what I can, I give Him – Give my heart.*

In the midst of a cold, hard hearted world – sometimes beautiful and sometimes bleak – be sure to give what is yours to truly give, something more than enough, not very costly, and likely valued by the recipient in ways that you may not understand, and may never know.

Chapter 14

Oh, How Joyfully – O du fröliche

Text: Johann D. Falk, 1816
Music: Anonymous, O *Sanctissima*

When we arrive on the third Sunday of Advent, it is time for joy! So I give you another old German hymn that celebrates Christmas Eve with rejoicing. The English words of this one express how we wait hopefully, sleep peacefully, and awake thankful for the shining light that is about to arrive. All of this, done joyfully, is something to celebrate.

Knowing this makes the origins of this carol very interesting. The tune was originally a Sicilian Mariners' song with words that were a prayer for blessings; a request for peace, joy, and a sense of being refreshed when travelling in the wilderness. German philosopher and poet, Johan Gottfried von Herder brought the melody back to Germany after travelling to Italy in 1788. Around 1816, the German lyrics were added by Johann Falk and it became one of the most popular *Weinachtslieder* (Christmas songs, for my English friends!). What is interesting about Falk, is that he was known as the Weimar orphan father. After losing four of his own children to typhoid fever, he founded an orphanage for abandoned children. This song was one he dedicated to these children.

Again, I am amazed at the resilience of the human spirit. Surely fishermen who sang this prayer were faced with challenging situations – stormy waters, hard work, and time away from family. Not an easy life in the 18th century. Yet they sang out of a desire to be filled with joy and peace. The "orphan father" had lost his children and was still able to rejoice with the orphans he cared for and encouraged. I read the English words of this carol and wonder if Christmas really means all it should to me. Do I value joy in the way that the original singers of this hymn do? I think I'd like to. But it does sometimes feel that our understanding of joy is confused by an insistence that happiness equals having everything we desire. I suspect that misses the mark on this one. Joy isn't really about possessions, success, or the details of our lives. It's about seeing possibilities. It's about choosing to be joyful. It's about grace.

So, in its long existence, this tune has been offered as a prayer for safety by fishermen, a children's song to encourage those orphaned by a plague, and a Christmas carol celebrating the arrival of a Saviour. The common thread in all of these is joy. Its importance. Its value. Let us look for it and then allow it to fill our lives.

O du fröliche ...
Oh, how joyfully ...
Riemire I nostril cuori di gioia e pace ...
Fill our hearts with joy and peace ...

Chapter 15

Lo, How A Rose E'er Blooming – *Es ist ein Ros' entsprungen*

Text: Anonymous, *Alte Catholische Geistliche Kirkengesang*, 1599
Music: *Alte Catholische Geistliche Kirkengesang*, 1599

The fourth Sunday of Advent is a celebration of love. This 15th century carol beautifully portrays the gift of a baby, the mother who bears him, and the sweet fragrance that fills the air upon his birth.

> *Lo, how a rose e'er blooming,*
> *From tender stem hath sprung!*
> *Of Jesse's lineage coming*
> *As men of old have sung.*
> *It came, a flow'ret bright,*
> *Amid the cold of winter,*
> *When half spent was the night.*

We are reminded that this is an act of love that brings us the fulfillment of a prophecy of old.

> *Isaiah 'twas foretold it,*
> *The Rose I have in mind.*
> *With Mary we behold it,*

The virgin mother kind.
To show God's love aright,
She bore to us a Savior,
When half spent was the night.

These words remind us that this is a moment where our humanity and God meet and become one. This union offers us an opportunity to bring light into a dark world.

Flower, whose fragrance tender
With sweetness fills the air,
Dispel with glorious splendour
The darkness everywhere.
True man, yet very God,
From Sin and death he saves us,
And lightens every load.

This is a carol that has been sung by both Catholic and Protestant traditions for hundreds of years. There is some variation in the word 'rose' in the original German. Some versions use *Ros'* as in the flower itself, a mystical kind of representation of Mary. Others use the word *Reis* which means a branch and speaks to the tree of Jesse, or his lineage. Either way, we are talking about a beautiful tribute to the belief that Jesus was born in a context – a particular place and time. A tribute within a history of a people waiting for a saviour, birthing this saviour and then welcoming him and all he represented. This is not so different from what many of us experience as we welcome new lives into our families or communities and watch them blossom and grow.

Can the example of this generous love carry us through this week? Whether we are with those we love or not? I don't know. Although these are beautiful words, they are not the whole story. I think that we can assume Mary's path was not so easy given the circumstances of her pregnancy. There were certainly many challenges facing this tiny baby, many that would not have felt filled with love. I think we know that countless people find themselves feeling unloved, unable to love or missing loved ones during this season. Maybe that's why the tune of this carol is so melancholic. Yes, the love displayed in God's gift can be seen as glorious, but the space in which we accept that gift may not be. So we continue to sing and hear this haunting love song. May its words help lighten the load, or simply accompany you as you continue to carry whatever life has given you.

Chapter 16

Go Tell It On The Mountain

Text: African American Spiritual, c. 1865
Music: African American Spiritual, c. 1865

I promise, this is it for Christmas – but I had one more to fit in from my list! This carol seemed to be a fitting way to bring the season to a close because what makes more sense than to share the news after a great event has taken place?

> *Go tell it on the mountain,*
> *over the hills and everywhere;*
> *go tell it on the mountain,*
> *that Jesus Christ is born.*

This is an African-American Spiritual dating back to the late 1800's, although a precise history of the hymn isn't really available. Some think it was written by Frederick Jerome Work, a black composer, teacher, and scholar; and then published by his son John Wesley Work in the 1907 anthology, *Folk Songs of the American Negro*. Others feel that John Work simply recorded an older spiritual for the first time. Either way, it probably started its life being sung by people who rarely had their voices heard. People who were not even allowed to have a voice. And yet, here is a song that is filled with joy, celebration and faith. Its origins are incredible when put in context.

To me, this kind of sums up what Christmas is: a time of celebration and joy mixed with sadness, contradiction, and sometimes disappointment. For some, it is a time for reviewing the foundations of a belief system. For others, it is a time to renew relationships and celebrate family. In amongst all of that, for many it brings to the surface reminders of loneliness, loss, and pain. If we stop to consider the historical context of the African American Spiritual in the late 1800s, we find a people emerging from a civil war with newfound freedoms – a cause for celebration. Yet, this emergence was fraught with conflict, danger, and challenges that continue to this day. The example provided by these old songs is powerful. The ability to sing despite the challenges is inspirational. The deep desire to move beyond circumstances that were and are beyond one's control brings tears to my eyes because of its strength and courage. The faith relied upon to do this is more than I can really understand, and it is something to be considered.

When I am a seeker,
I seek both night and day;
I seek the Lord to help me,
and He shows me the way:
Go tell it on the mountain,

over the hills and everywhere;
go tell it on the mountain,
that Jesus Christ is born.

As we shift past all the festivities of this season, I come away with a renewed sense that music provides something very powerful. I see it in this Spiritual and have seen it in so many places over the past few weeks. The words and tunes that are so familiar and longstanding are that way for a reason. I am reminded of a video that was circulating on the internet recently. An older Jewish woman was singing to an African American Alzheimer's patient. As she sang "He's Got the Whole World In His Hands" there was suddenly a recognition from deep inside someone whose voice had been lost, and this lovely woman started to sing along. Here two women shared a beautiful moment, and it didn't matter at all that they were of different faiths, they simply enabled each other to sing together despite the circumstances. So I leave you with this, let us sing it together.

He's got the whole world in his hands;
She's got the whole world in her hands;
We've got the whole world in our hands.

Merry Christmas.

Chapter 17

Worship The Lord In The Beauty Of Holiness

Text: John S. B. Monsell, *Hymns of Love & Praise*, 1863
Music: *Manuscript Chorale Book*, 1754

In early January, we celebrate Epiphany. Well, the church does. I must admit that by this point in the holidays I am usually relaxing fairly seriously and have rarely, if ever, made it to a church service. So I had to look this up to figure out what Epiphany actually was. I had some vague notion of it having to do with the wise men arriving, or us all coming to some understanding of what this Christ child was, but that's about the extent of my knowledge. I wasn't way off, because it is traditionally the festival that celebrates the moment when it is revealed that Christ is God born as a human being, and this revelation is made to the three Magi.

Not surprisingly, I didn't receive any requests for a favourite hymn that matches with this day. There are not very many of them to begin with, and I suspect it isn't a high point in the liturgical year for most of us. And yet, it is a fairly spectacular concept – the merging of the Divine with humanity. As I thought about it, I wondered if it shouldn't be more important to me. The idea that as a human I am worthy of this deep connection with God; that I am, in a sense, part of this spiritual union, is powerful. Once again it speaks to our intrinsic value.

The hymn I chose to reflect upon for this day, is a beautiful tune from the mid 1700s, with text written by John S. B. Monsell around 1863. The words that struck me most were these:

Fear not to enter his courts in the slenderness
of the poor wealth thou wouldst reckon as thine;
truth in its beauty, and love in its tenderness,
these are the offerings to lay on His shrine.

These, though we bring them
in trembling and fearfulness,
he will accept for the Name that is dear;
mornings of joy give for evenings of tearfulness,
trust for our trembling, and hope for our fear.

We live in a world where what is valued revolves heavily around success, fame, money, appearances, and possessions. There seems to be a very short list of gifts and talents that are deemed worthy of celebration, or even acceptance. But these words remind me that it is truth and love that are welcome. In moments of discouragement and perceived failure, these remain — even if brought forward with fear and trembling. When thinking about this moment of epiphany, of this discovery that we are worthy of being connected to the Divine, we need to recognize that the gifts to be offered are within us. We need not acquire them, and we need not even be confident as we give them. To me this is so hopeful, sacred, and shared by us all. This is the union of our humanness and divinity and the beauty of holiness.

Chapter 18

Guide Me, O Thou Great Jehovah

Text: William Williams, *Aleluiam*, 1745
Music: John Hughes, 1905/7

Whenever we find ourselves at the start of a new year it seems like a good time to review the past, to think about the future, and to embrace the present. A few people recommended this hymn to me, and I found it in the section of my hymnbook categorized *Faith Journey: Suffering/Joy*. To me that probably sums up what many of us consider at the start of a new year regardless of the specifics of our faith or spiritual leanings. I like that it is about both suffering and joy, because it often seems like we focus too much one way or the other and lose sight of the reality that we are rarely bereft of one whilst in the company of the other.

When I asked for favourite hymns, a friend included this note. She wrote, "This hymn was sung at the funeral of each of my parents. They were people who were so conscious of the guidance of God, whether in the smallest aspects of life or in the big decisions and crises." The poetic text reflects this beautifully.

Guide me, O thou great Jehovah,
pilgrim through this barren land.
I am weak, but thou art mighty;
hold me with thy pow'rful hand.
Bread of Heaven, Bread of Heaven,
feed me till I want no more,
feed me till I want no more.

Open now the crystal fountain
whence the healing waters flow.
Let the fiery, cloudy pillar
lead me all my journey through.
Strong Deliv'rer, strong Deliv'rer,
I will ever give to thee, I will ever give to thee.

When I tread the verge of Jordan,
bid my anxious fears subside.
Death of death and hell's destruction,
land me safe on Canaan's side.
Songs of praises, songs of praises,
I will ever give to thee, I will ever give to thee.

This has been a popular hymn since 1907 when John Hughes reworked his 1905 tune for the inauguration of the organ in Capel Rhondda in Wales. This chapel celebrated its 150th anniversary in 2003 with the playing and singing of this hymn tune known as *Cwm Rhondda*. It has apparently also become the unofficial anthem of Welsh Rugby! Stories of its singing at celebrations abound, including the wedding of Prince William and Kate Middleton. But again, the song reminds us of the duality of life's experiences because it was also sung at Prince William's mother Diana's funeral. This ability to encompass both joy and sorrow is why I love hymns. For me, they sometimes arouse mixed feelings. Music stirs emotions despite the words that I grapple with; or perhaps it is the words that inspire and music that doesn't. Of course, these songs we sing are filled with memories of people, places, and experiences.

As we move into and through each new year and begin to create new memories, I hope that you experience more joy than sorrow. But if that is not what life brings you, then I hope you find your Bread of Heaven; something that helps carry, sustain, and guide you; something that allows you to surround yourself with Songs of Praises.

Chapter 19

Trust And Obey

Text: John H. Sammis, *Hymns Old and New*, 1887
Music: Daniel B. Towner, *Hymns Old and New* 1887

This is a special hymn because it was given to me by my father-in-law as a favourite filled with memories and life-long meaning. I don't think he will mind me sharing his story, and once again it is a reminder of how long-lasting the impact of some of these hymns can be. He recalls that as a child he observed his grandfather baptizing people outdoors and as each person emerged from the water, those gathered would sing a verse of this song. What an image: rising from the waters of this spiritual rite and hearing your community singing in support of your faith.

> *When we walk with the Lord*
> *In the light of His Word,*
> *What a glory He sheds on our way;*
> *While we do His good will,*
> *He abides with us still,*
> *And with all who will trust and obey.*

I was so struck by the powerful image of a young boy observing an elder family member practice his faith in a very real and meaningful way. This child, looking upon a spiritual leader, grew into a man who holds the memory of this demonstration dear in his heart. More than sixty years later it was still powerful enough to share. I think that there is a lesson in this for all of us. We have little idea of what long-term impact our behaviour and actions have on the children around us. We can't see into the future how an afternoon's memory will carry someone throughout their life. We can't predict which demonstration of our beliefs and values will be the thing that sustains others through challenges, or perhaps, prepares one for being the sustainer.

But we never can prove
The delights of his love
Until all on the altar we lay;
For the favor he shows,
For the joy he bestows,
Are for them who will trust and obey.

When I sat down to work on this hymn, I found myself reflecting on both the simplicity and depth of this childhood experience. But I also heard a kind of flying in its tune; sailing up from the waters and representing a life guided firmly by one's values; carried carefully by one's faith. I understand that this means something different to each of us, but our ability to sow the seeds of memory that may grow into life-long sustenance requires us all to find and stand on solid ground. My hope is that this song will remind you of someone who gave you that kind of experience as a child. Or, perhaps, be a reminder that in your actions, small and large, you may be giving something that sixty years from now will be remembered, shared, and treasured.

Chapter 20

O Power of Love

Text: Gerhard Tersteegen, 1757
Music: Dmitri S. Bortniansky, *Choralbuch*, 1825

I'm learning that, for those of us who grew up in the church, there are all sorts of stories that emerge when we think of these hymns. They mean something different to each of us, but it seems that the experience of remembering these tunes or words is something we share. Interesting. I keep coming back to the idea that music can serve as a means of unifying us despite our differences, and this sharing of memories – both precious and amusing – is sort of encouraging to me.

Why amusing? Well, this week's hymn was given to me by an aunt who shared another childhood memory with me. I found it quite funny, but maybe one has to have the benefit of being in the same situation to fully appreciate it! She wrote, "I can still hear the older ladies in my childhood church singing at the tops of their voices to hit the high notes. The range did not discourage them from singing as loud as they could!" Funny because I have certainly been in the situation of hearing people belt out a high note out of sheer enthusiasm with little concern for whether the note could actually be reached. There is a temptation to cringe. But, there is also a part of me that admires those who sing with complete abandon because they believe in the words or simply love singing.

The text of this hymn was written by Gerhard Tersteegen in the early 1700s. He was raised in the Reformed Church in Germany, but left the church to pursue his own spirituality as a mystic and leader of a small group of "awakened souls" who were devoted to meditation and translation of the works of earlier mystics and quietists. The words of the first verse bring to mind the transcendent experience of singing with abandon, of being committed to one's truth regardless of the conventions or trends surrounding us – kind of how Tersteegen lived his spiritual life.

> *O pow'r of love, all else transcending,*
> *In Jesus present evermore,*
> *I worship Thee, in homage bending,*
> *Thy name to honor and adore.*
> *Yea, let my soul, in deep devotion,*
> *Bathe in love's mighty, boundless ocean.*

Bathe in love's mighty, boundless ocean. Wow. To find my soul in that space sort of diminishes any requirement to worry about hitting a high note. Although, it also requires me to seek out the best high note possible. This is a powerful image inspiring both courageous confidence and the pursuit of excellence. Singing at the top of our voices, whether an older lady or not, is an honour and a gift. It means we've really committed to whatever it is that grounds us; settled in to wherever we find love's boundless ocean. So, regardless of what form your voice takes, sing.

Chapter 21

Just A Closer Walk With Thee

Text: Anonymous, mid 1800s
Music: Anonymous, mid 1800s

We come to the rock star of our hymns this week. A tune that has been recorded by a dizzying array of artists consistently since 1941. Everyone from Mahalia Jackson, Louis Armstrong, Patsy Cline, Ella Fitzgerald, Elvis Presley, Merle Haggard, Harry Connick Jr., Joan Baez, Bob Dylan, Van Morrison, Lawrence Welk, The Fray, and Eric Clapton have recorded and performed it – and many more! What is it about this one that has made it so popular?

It's an old gospel song, said to have its roots in the southern African American church and in the field singing of slaves. Although it may have originated prior to the American Civil War, the version we're probably most familiar with is the one from the 1940s when it was first recorded. There is no known author of the text, although a few people have added to and adjusted the lyrics over the years.

This is a very personal prayer and a song filled with the desire to be carried by something beyond our own strength. It includes an acknowledgement of our weakness, burdens, and need for support.

I am weak, but Thou art strong,
Jesus, keep me from all wrong,
I'll be satisfied as long As I walk,
let me walk close to Thee.

Through this world of toil and snares,
If I falter, Lord, who cares?
Who with me my burden shares?
None but Thee, dear Lord, none but Thee.

When my feeble life is o'er,
Time for me will be no more,
Guide me gently, safely o'er
To Thy kingdom's shore, to Thy shore.

Maybe that's why it has been so popular. I suppose that we all struggle with our inability to manage everything. We all live in a world filled with toil and snares – things that derail our plans and best intentions. We all have moments where we feel like our lives are feeble. These insecurities and challenges are common and even the most successful among us face them. The specifics of whom we look to as a supportive walking partner may vary, but we're all looking. My wish is that you find that partner – be they earthly or spiritual.

Walk closely together. Guide and be guided gently and safely to the shore on the other side.

> *Just a closer walk with thee,*
> *grant it, Jesus, is my plea,*
> *daily walking close to thee:*
> *Let it be, dear Lord, let it be.*

Chapter 22

When Peace, Like A River

Text: Horatio G. Spafford, *Gospel Hymns, No. 2*, 1876
Music: Philip P. Bliss, *Gospel Hymns, No. 2*, 1876

We have arrived at one of our most treasured hymns. I think that it may be the one on my list that was most often suggested. One friend shared, "This hymn is my mom in all circumstances." What a statement. What an image of a strong and caring woman for a daughter to look up to. What great expressions of love by both the demonstrator and observer of this kind of strength.

> *When peace, like a river, attendeth my way,*
> *When sorrows like sea billows roll;*
> *Whatever my lot, Thou has taught me to say,*
> *It is well, it is well, with my soul.*

And on it goes, repeating the phrase "it is well with my soul" until we start to feel that this seemingly impossible spiritual state is, in fact, possible.

This is a hymn born out of tragedy. The story is quite famous. After suffering financial ruin following the Chicago Fire of 1871, Horatio G. Spafford sent his family to Europe while he cleaned up the mess. The ship they were travelling on was involved in a collision and all four of his daughters died. It was when he passed near the spot of their death that he wrote these words. The tune, written later by Philip P. Bliss, is named *Ville du Havre*, after the ill-fated ship.

Once again, I am amazed at what emerges from tragedy, and how some special souls in our world seem to be able to express, through the deepest pain, something that serves to inspire and uplift us – over time and through generations. The ability to both share and rise above our pain brought me a number of stories about singing this hymn at funerals. It moves us, makes us weep, helps us grieve, and gives us comfort. What struck me, however, was that it is often those who are dying that give us these words of comfort by requesting they be sung. This is a song that allows those left behind to feel assurance. These are words that, when given, allow us to send our loved ones to their eternal rest. That is an enormous gift.

And Lord, haste the day
when my faith shall be sight,
The clouds be rolled back as a scroll;
The trump shall resound,
and the Lord shall descend,
Even so, it is well with my soul.

I get choked up every time I sing "the trump shall resound" because it is a magnificent image. It implies a welcome of great proportions. It's the kind of welcome I think we would all like. It's certainly what we wish for those who go before us. Whether sung at a funeral or not, this hymn brings us to a sacred place of contemplating our soul's wellness, and a place where we can choose to lovingly express and share the deepest strength of our being. Perhaps that lies in faith; perhaps in choices, integrity, values, relationships, inspiration, beauty, or simply contemplation. I wish that, like my friend's mother, these words described me in all circumstances, and maybe one day they will. But even more, I hope that I can find the part of me that will give these words to those I love when the time comes that they need them. Those who have done so are beyond inspiring.

> *It is well, with my soul,*
> *It is well, with my soul,*
> *It is well, it is well, with my soul.*

Chapter 23

Go, My Children

Text: Sir Harold Boulton, 1884: Jaroslav J. Vajda, 1983
Music: Welsh Fold Melody

It is time to enter the season of Lent. For those within the Christian Church, this is a season of reflection and preparation. It is a time when we contemplate our spiritual state and consider how this is reflected by our actions. When I looked at the traditional meaning of Lent, I found that there is a three-pronged approach to the practices many undertake during this time. These are actually centred on the idea of justice. First, prayer represents justice towards God. Fasting (self-denial) represents justice towards the self. Finally, almsgiving represents the justice we show to our neighbours. To me, this seems to be a more holistic approach than the gloomy 'give things up' idea I often associate with this period. It speaks to our spirit, body, and community. It is interesting to note that even in the world outside of the Christian church, people are starting to consider the value of this time as well – a time to meditate, think about environmental stewardship and personal health. For many, Lent designates a time to consciously reflect.

This is a time of personal reflection. The music is contemplative, some might say melancholy and sad. It is a quiet time. And as such, it can be lonely. So I picked this hymn as a reminder that while, in many ways, deeply personal reflection is a solitary act, we are not alone. There is something beyond us that carries, feeds and fills us. For some of us that is God. For some it is the love of our families and friends. For some it lies in the natural word. For some of us it is something that we don't really understand or even know how to define. I do acknowledge that for some it can feel like there is no source for this deep strength, this river of love.

So while this hymn reminds me of the care I receive, perhaps it can also give me guidance in providing this blessing to those who can't find it. Maybe Lent isn't so much about thinking of things to give up. Maybe it's about thinking of the many ways we can give.

> *Go, my children, with my blessing, never alone.*
> *Waking, sleeping, I am with you,*
> *you are my own.*
> *In my love's baptismal river,*
> *I have made you mine forever.*
> *Go, my children, with my blessing;*
> *you are my own.*

Go, my children, fed and nourished,
closer to me.
Grow in love and love by serving,
joyful and free.
Here my Spirit's power filled you,
here his tender comfort stilled you.
Go, my children, fed and nourished,
joyful and free.

Chapter 24

Take Thou My Hand, O Father – So nimm den meine Hände

Text: Julie K. Hausmann, *Maiblumen Lieder einer Stillen im Lande*, 1862
Music: Friedrich Silcher, *Kinderlieder, Vol. III*, 1918

> *Take Thou my hand, O Father,*
> *and lead Thou me,*
> *Until my journey endeth eternally.*
> *Alone I will not wander one single day.*
> *Be Thou my true companion and with me stay.*

As we continue to walk through the season of Lent, I'm finding that the hymns I was given have a common link in that they all address the idea of being alone. Words that remind us that while we live in community, we face our spiritual challenges alone; we face ourselves and our God alone. However, we can find deep and meaningful solace in the companionship that comes from walking towards whatever is our foundation. It's something that becomes possible when we trust the goodness that results in standing on solid ground despite the sense of shakiness that life sometimes provides.

Though naught of Thy great power
may move my soul,
With Thee through night and darkness
I reach the goal.
Take, then, my hands, O Father,
and lead Thou me,
Until my journey endeth eternally.

This is an old German hymn that a few people said brought them to tears whenever they heard it. It is a reminder of the examples of strength some saw in their parents' and grandparents' lives. It is a prayer for strength in our own lives. It is an acknowledgement that we cannot, and perhaps do not, walk alone – even if we feel profound loneliness, there is something beyond us that can hold our hands along the journey.

So nimm denn meine Hände und führe mich
Bis an mein selig Ende und ewiglich!
Ich kann allein nicht gehen, nicht einen Schritt;
Wo du wirst gehn und stehen, da nimm mich mit.

These words were written by the Baltic German poet Julie Katharina von Hausmann around 1864. Legend has it that she was engaged to a theology student on a mission whom she travelled to Africa to wed. Upon her arrival, she found that he had died from a tropical fever. It's hard to imagine this in our time of instant communication, but travel in 1864 with this news waiting must have been completely devastating and disorienting. She returned to Latvia after this tragedy and spent the remainder of her life working with the poor and writing poetry. Her work was published during her lifetime under the condition that it be done anonymously and that all profits go to an orphanage in Hong Kong.

Again, here is an example of tremendous strength in the face of overwhelming tragedy. An example of what must have been an incredibly lonely journey resulting in such giving, and such selflessness. An example of knowing to ask for a hand to help lead the way. We all face a variety of challenges; some shared, some private. Finding something or someone, to hold a hand while we do so is a blessing. Being able to ask for that hand might just be a sign of deep understanding, humility, and strength. The hands we hold are a real treasure, and our ability to see these hands is a gift.

Chapter 25

Give Me Jesus

Text: African American Spiritual
Music: African American Spiritual

I love Spirituals. They are so filled with story and emotion. They have hidden meanings and deep pain, faith, and strength. And they are often such beautiful, simple tunes that can evoke so much feeling. I couldn't find much information on this one, other than many variations of the words, but there is an explanation of it that I found revealing.

It is said to be a reference to what was left to the freed slaves after the American Civil War. In other words, in a state of extreme poverty and an absence of worldly possessions or the means to earn a living, the words "you can have all this world" may have been a criticism of their treatment following this apparent victory.

Give me Jesus,
Give me Jesus,
You can have all this world,
Give me Jesus.

I chose to think of this one as a Lenten hymn because it continues with the theme of facing our spiritual journey alone. We must all come to terms with how to do that and how, specifically, we will face the ultimate personal experience of death. This is not something we like to talk about, but it is something that we all carry in common.

Oh, when I am alone,
Oh, when I am alone,
Oh, when I am alone,
Give me Jesus.

Oh, when I come to die,
Oh, when I come to die,
Oh, when I come to die,
Give me Jesus.

It really is a testament to someone's faith or spiritual strength to sing words like these. To be so confident in the source of strength even in the darkest, loneliest moment, is very moving. It is inspiring. I suspect it is rare. I think we spend our lives searching for that personal confidence and strength – hoping to have it when our time arrives. I'm pretty sure I've been hearing this song and its ideas since my Sunday School days, but I think the secret to this kind of deep faith and spiritual strength lies in what we do every day. The strength that carries us through challenges is built by our choices and built over time. Perhaps looking for it every morning allows us to be comforted by it in the evening, and to be carried by it through the night. What a thing to learn from those freed slaves. What a legacy for us to honour.

In the morning when I rise,
In the morning when I rise,
In the morning when I rise,
Give me Jesus.

Chapter 26

What Wondrous Love Is This

Text: Anonymous, *Cluster of Spiritual Songs*, 1823
Music: American Folk Hymn, *Southern Harmony*, 1840

As I wandered through the season of Lent, it took a while to get to an actual Lenten hymn. Here it is, although, the history of it didn't exactly match up with my expectations of a hymn that is quite commonly heard at this time of year. The words were first published around 1811 as a camp song and are sometimes attributed to Methodist minister Alexander Means, but it is unclear if he actually wrote them. The music, however, has a more interesting story. There are many examples in early church music (when it was unusual for people to be able to read words or notes), where it was common to set religious words to a popular tune for ease of learning and appeal. This is one of those hymns. It is the same tune as the English song *The Ballad of Captain Kidd* (c.1701), which describes the exploits of pirate William Kidd. It may even predate that, and apparently there were at least a dozen popular songs to this tune at the time. So, a pretty gloomy camp song, with pirate music ends up being a Lenten standard. I guess we never know where things may end up!

I was quite pleased that someone suggested this hymn to me. I've always loved its haunting tune and the way the words repeat in order to get the point across, adding weight with each repetition, and becoming heavier and heavier until we all start to sing, bearing this weight together, by the millions.

What wondrous love is this,
O my soul, O my soul!
What wondrous love is this, O my soul!
What wondrous love is this that caused
the Lord of bliss
To bear the dreadful curse for my soul,
for my soul,
To bear the dreadful curse for my soul.

When I was sinking down, sinking down,
sinking down,
When I was sinking down, sinking down,
When I was sinking down
beneath God's righteous frown,
Christ laid aside His crown for my soul,
for my soul,
Christ laid aside His crown for my soul.

To God and to the Lamb, I will sing, I will sing;
To God and to the Lamb, I will sing.
To God and to the Lamb

Who is the great "I Am";
While millions join the theme,
I will sing, I will sing;
While millions join the theme, I will sing.

Maybe this one is a turning point in my Lenten theme of aloneness. Maybe as we face our spiritual journeys alone, we have the choice to do so in the company of many. Multitudes of different voices, words, ideas, and perspectives all singing for strength and comfort. Whether we are singing in solitary praise or in community, I take comfort in it. It is what moves me when I sing many of these hymns despite concerns that I may have over some of the words; some of the church's history; some of my own pain as a result of conflict and struggle within the church. There is something to be said for joining our voices together in song. To sing with the millions — regardless of who or where they are — is a magnificent example of the ideal of wondrous love. So we sing, campers and pirates alike. And when we do, we are all carried by the strength of a million voices.

Chapter 27

Ah, Holy Jesus

Text: Johann Heermann, *Devoti Musica Cordis*, 1630
Music: Johann Crüger, *Neues vollkömliches Gesangbuch*, Vol. II, 1640

Our journey through Lent continues with one of my favourite hymn tunes. Another beautifully haunting melody, it has been used many times in its almost 400-year history to express the deeply personal experience of acknowledging one's humanity in light of a Divine gift; the sacrifice of one in aid of another. The example of providing for someone in need at great cost, regardless of what is deserved.

> *Ah, holy Jesus, how hast thou offended,*
> *that mortal judgement hath on thee descended?*
> *By foes derided, by thine own rejected,*
> *O most afflicted!*

The words, written by Johann Heerman in 1630, were published in his collection entitled *Devoti Musica Cordis*, or music for a devout heart. This book of poetic hymn texts was subtitled as *Haus und Hertz-musica* (music for home and heart), and was meant for personal not public use. These words were not for public proclamations, they were for quiet, internal reflection.

Who was the guilty?
Who brought this upon thee?
Alas, my treason, Jesus, hath undone thee!
'Twas I, Lord Jesus, I it was denied thee;
I crucified thee.

This is difficult subject matter. I think that no matter what you believe or how you interpret the details in these words, acknowledging one's own culpability for that which is wrong is challenging. Facing up to our individual responsibility towards what is evil, unethical, or immoral, is hard. Finding a way through the darkness that exists, whether we choose to look at it or not, is unpleasant. It requires us to look at both our action and inaction with different eyes than the ones that are comfortably ours.

And yet, there is a light to be found in the looking. I am often surprised to find that facing darkness is a way to see light. It sounds a bit corny, but the light at the end of the tunnel can only be found because we were courageous enough to walk through the tunnel. This hymn speaks to the undeserved salvation that Christ gives, a belief many hold dear. But it also provides a glimpse into the idea that undeserved kindness and love brings us to the light, both as givers and receivers. So while we face the darkness in our world and hope in doing so, to find our salvation, we also have an opportunity to shed light on the path for others along the way, not because any of us deserve it, but simply because the light exists.

> *Therefore, kind Jesus, since I cannot pay thee,*
> *I do adore thee, and will ever pray thee,*
> *think on thy pity and thy love unswerving,*
> *not my deserving.*

Chapter 28

O Sacred Head, Now Wounded

Text: Paul Gerhardt, *Praxis Pietatis Melica*, 1656
Music: Hans L. Hassler, *Lustgarten neuer Deutscher Gesäng*, 1601

The final Sunday of Lent marks the beginning of a week in which the church contemplates the Passion of Christ. The term "passion" is one we hear tossed about quite frequently – as in, follow your passion or find your passion. It does mean to feel something deeply, but it actually comes from the Greek word πάσχειν (*paschein*) which means to suffer. This resonates with the symbolism found in the story of Christ's triumphal entry into Jerusalem, the Last Supper, his agonizing time in the Garden of Gethsemane and his arrest, trial and crucifixion. It's a story of suffering – a quick fall to the lowest of places.

This hymn is sometimes known as the Passion Hymn. Its words are based on a medieval poem, usually attributed to Bernard of Clairvaux, in which the various verses address the different parts of Christ's body hanging on the cross. The text we are familiar with comes from the verse speaking of Christ's head.

O sacred head, now wounded,
with grief and shame weighed down,
now scornfully surrounded
with thorns, your only crown!
O sacred head, what glory,
what bliss till now was thine!
Yet, though despised and gory,
I joy to call thee mine.

The music was written by Hans Leo Hassler in 1601 and was harmonized by Bach in 1729. It has been used many, many times in musical commemorations of the Passion story, and also simply as a beautiful tune. Bach arranged five stanzas in his *St. Matthew Passion*, Liszt included an arrangement in his *Via Crucis*, and Paul Simon's *American Tune* is based on this hymn.

There is a difficult beauty to this hymn. The tune is of a stunning loveliness and filled with heartbreaking melancholy. The words are hard to read, and harder to sing. This is an emotionally charged work that can stir so much feeling, and so many questions. I love this hymn and yet I am disturbed by it when I allow myself to take in the words. There is suffering, there is pain, there is guilt, there is confusion, and a little anger, and there is love. This example of carrying someone else's burdens so they don't have to, is powerful. How can we possibly apply this model to our own lives? I'm not sure, but I suspect that it is necessary to try. What a gift to offer. What a gift to receive.

> *What language shall I borrow*
> *to thank thee, dearest friend,*
> *for this, thy dying sorrow,*
> *thy pity without end?*
>
> *O make me thine forever,*
> *and should I fainting be,*
> *Lord, let me never, never,*
> *outlive my love to thee.*

Chapter 29

Were You There?

Text: African American Spiritual, *Old Plantation Hymns*, 1899
Music: African American Spiritual, *Folksongs of the American Negro*, 1907

This spiritual was first published in 1899, but is thought to predate the American Civil War. It is another slave song, and it is interesting to note that it is the first spiritual to be included in a major American hymnal (Episcopal Church Hymnal, 1940). The song has remained a staple in the church ever since, and is particularly sung on Good Friday.

The words are haunting. The tune is haunting. It brings to our minds a haunting event. Yes, it tells of the death of Christ on the cross, but what else were the slaves singing about? I kind of think it requires me to think about the many "crucifixions" that happen every day around our world, both near and far. Do I tremble when others are sacrificed? Do I consider being present when it happens? What role do I play in others' suffering? And so I leave it with you to consider.

Were you there when they crucified my Lord?
Were you there when they crucified my Lord?
Oh! Sometimes it causes me to tremble!
tremble! tremble!
Were you there when they crucified my Lord?

Chapter 30

Low In The Grave He Lay

Text: Robert Lowry, 1874
Music: Robert Lowry, 1874

Easter. I suppose it is the most significant day on the liturgical calendar, and I know many people celebrate it in traditional ways with rousing church services and family gatherings. For those who celebrate in these ways, I wish you a Happy Easter. For those who don't, I offer you a slightly different Easter experience! The hymn for today comes courtesy of my sister, and if you know her, it will be amusing that she has provided the Easter selection. But, as I've been reminded many times, these hymns carry our stories with them and this one is part of my family's tale.

Imagine yourself on a family car trip. The long drives, the cramped quarters of an old station wagon and the endless attempt to find some entertainment for the three kids in the back seat. Imagine that the passengers come from a singing tradition and the kids are just slightly odd. Bingo. You have a recipe for some spectacular singing of *Low In The Grave He Rose*. Loudly, boisterously and in some kind of harmony; but perhaps not always with the exact words as found in the hymnal (nose and hose do, in fact, rhyme with arose...). I suspect my sister's recommendation comes with a similar humorous memory, and I'm guessing that our parents have blocked it out.

So many of the hymns I've been given to reflect upon are bringing back memories for me (and I hope for you as well); memories of experiences and sometimes of people. For me, that is what makes them such treasures. The music and words take us to places we've been before. But they can also bring us somewhere new. I suppose that Easter is about what is new – new life, rebirth – and it fits neatly into our choice to celebrate it in Spring. This hymn has always seemed a bit cheesy to me; the over-the-top melodrama of starting slow and solemn and then bursting forth into a rousing chorus. But maybe that's the point. Winter is bleak, spring brings new life. Applying this to the Christian understanding of the Easter story is pretty easy – after death comes the resurrection.

Low in the grave he lay, Jesus my Savior, waiting the coming day, Jesus my Lord!

*Up from the grave he arose;
with a mighty triumph o'er his foes;
he arose a victor from the dark domain,
and he lives forever, with his saints to reign.
He arose! He arose! Hallelujah! Christ arose!*

I look back on my family car trips with fondness. We saw many new things. We argued and we had fun. We read, we played games, we ignored each other, we fought over the borders found on the car's seats, and we sang. And we sang, and we sang. Easter reminds me of our singing. Not just in the car, but everywhere. For me, singing is refreshing. It allows my spirit to emerge renewed. I suppose that this can also be part of the Easter story. This experience of finding renewal through the voices we've been given. Through the sharing of our experiences. With our families – those we were born into and those we've chosen. Hallelujah!

Chapter 31

And Can It Be That I Should Gain?

Text: Charles Wesley, *Psalms and Hymns*, 1738
Music: Thomas Campbell, *The Bouquet*, 1825

It is no secret that Charles Wesley wrote many hymns, but until I started looking deeper into this particular one, I had no idea how many. It is reported that he wrote 6500 hymns in his lifetime. By my calculations, he would have had to write at least 80 hymns a year throughout his 81 years of life. Now, granted, some of them were probably less good than others, but still, he has earned the title of the "Bard of Methodism" for the fact that 623 of the 770 hymns in the Wesleyan Hymn Book were his. And let's not forget that he was inducted into the Gospel Music Hall of Fame in 1995! Quite an accomplishment and legacy.

This hymn is considered by many to be one of his best. I must admit that I hadn't heard or sung it in a long time, but it is indeed very familiar. Certainly, I remember singing it as a child. It was suggested to me by a friend who relates the story of learning to conduct it as a course requirement at Moody Bible Institute in Chicago. It may be her only conducting skill, but she claims she can fill in, in a pinch, on this one if needed!

The story goes that Wesley wrote these words in 1738 to celebrate his conversion experience.

And can it be that I should gain
An interest in the Savior's blood?
Died He for me, who caused His pain?
For me, who Him to death pursued?
Amazing love! How can it be
That Thou, my God, shouldst die for me?
Amazing love! How can it be
That Thou, my God, shouldst die for me?

He was a writer who used the hymn form to express his feelings on all sorts of experiences. Christian festivals, doctrine, personal experiences, natural disasters, historical events, scripture. Everything. And by the vast number of hymns he wrote, he obviously felt that he had much to say. I suppose self-expression is what music is about, and obviously musicians and lyricists still do that today, but I like that it's been going on forever, this need to speak through song. This desire to write and write and write what is in our hearts. What really interests me, however, is that he chose hymns to express himself. Hymn writers have an ability to share what is deep within and then they provide a space for others to take part in the experience, especially because singing hymns is a participatory act. Writing hymns is about getting others involved with the text and music, and there is an underlying assumption that they will not just be read or listened to. We are all invited to engage.

I love that we sing many of these hymns together. I love having a glimpse of someone's thoughts and feelings, whether I agree with or even understand every word. I love having the opportunity to participate. So, thank you Charles Wesley – and many others – for writing these songs we sing. It is an amazing act of love to have done so, whatever the motivation. To share these words and tunes with the generations is a gift that I am grateful for.

Chapter 32

O Perfect Love

Text: Dorothy F. Blomfield Gurney, 1883
Music: Joseph Barnby, *Church Hymnary*, 1898

I chose this hymn for a very special reason at a very special time. Fifty years earlier, this hymn had been sung at a wedding. It was the day my parents were married. Something to celebrate! As I look around my world, I notice that marriages seem as likely to fail as they are to succeed, and I think it is worth noting the ones that stand the test of time. I'm not sure why some succeed, and some don't. There are many, many reasons I'm sure, but this hymn's text acknowledges the challenges of this kind of relationship and this kind of commitment by offering a prayer for it; the need for something beyond our humanness to ensure endurance.

> *O perfect Love,*
> *all human thought transcending,*
> *lowly we kneel in prayer before thy throne,*
> *that theirs may be the love*
> *which knows no ending,*
> *whom thou in sacred vow dost join in one.*

O perfect Life, be thou their full assurance
of tender charity and steadfast faith,
of patient hope and quiet, brave endurance,
with childlike trust that fears no pain or death.

Grant them the joy
which brightens earthly sorrow;
grant them the peace
which calms all earthly strife;
grant them the vision
of the glorious morrow
that will reveal eternal love and life.

These words were written by Dorothy F. Blomfield in 1883 for her sister's wedding. I like that they reflect on the idea that this relationship – this life partnership – can help us through the sorrows and strife to be found in our lives. I like that the community gathered at the wedding participates in asking for the security of the sacred vow. This joining of individual commitment and communal support is probably a really important ingredient in successful relationships, one whose value we can underestimate in our busy lives and in times when diminished connections to any community are prevalent.

As I read these words, I am very conscious of those to whom it doesn't seem to apply. Those who are not married or, perhaps, differently married than what a hymn implies, including those who are single, by choice or not; and those who are separated, estranged or divorced from the one they made that sacred vow with. Personally, I choose to view these words in a broader sense than just the traditional description of a marriage. I think that there are many beautiful relationships to be found that can, and should, be supported by our communities; and many that can rely on the sacred nature of commitment and love to carry those involved through their entire lives. I value these kinds of deep, caring, loving relationships and friendships, and I wish them for everyone.

I am thankful that my parents chose to foster something that endured for years. I hope that the experience of observing a long, successful marriage reminds me of the value to be found in committing to something or someone this deeply. But I also hope that this foundation provides a space of compassion for those who have lost this thing that we celebrate. It is indeed a privilege to have a life partner. It is not always easy to find or keep one. We celebrate those who succeed – but let us also carry those who do not.

Chapter 33

Bless'd Be The Tie That Binds

Text: John Fawcett, *Hymns Adapted to the Circumstances of Public Worship*, 1782
Music: Johann G. Nägeli, adapted by Lowell Mason, *The Psaltery*, 1845

The week before I wrote this, there was a baptism at my church. It doesn't actually happen that often, and this one was quite moving. I suppose for some, that is always the case, but what made this so meaningful to me was the gratitude expressed by my friend as she spoke about the community she was being baptized into. It seemed that somehow her connections with various people in the congregation had opened up a space to find God in a way that was significant for her. The value of our communities has been a recurring theme for me as I look at all these hymns, and as I sat through that baptismal service, it was once again reinforced. This sacred rite took on new meaning for me as I received the gift of my friend's gratitude. I am thankful for that.

It is fitting that this hymn came up this week because it speaks of a kind of community that supports our spiritual lives. It speaks of fellowship that goes beyond socializing to something deeper.

Fellowship that is both life affirming and life supporting.

> *Bless'd be the tie that binds*
> *our hearts in Christian love;*
> *the fellowship of kindred minds*
> *is like to that above.*
>
> *Before our Father's throne*
> *we pour our ardent prayers;*
> *our fears, our hopes, our aims are one,*
> *our comforts and our cares.*
>
> *We share our mutual woes,*
> *our mutual burdens bear,*
> *and often for each other flows*
> *the sympathizing tear.*

What I like about these words is the commitment to sharing in the experiences of life together by pouring out our fears, our hopes, our aims, our cares. The flowing of a sympathetic tear is something I both see and experience often in my community. It may seem to be a small thing, but to know someone else will cry with you, and see your pain and your joy, is a powerful support. And a powerful draw to remain a part of the community. The author of these words, John Fawcett (1740-1817), apparently had the experience of being compelled to stay with his congregation by the love and tears of the people – all after he had given his farewell sermon and loaded his cart to move to a new post! Community support can mean everything to us amidst lives that are chaotic, stressful, challenging, pain-filled, joyful, happy and exciting. Whatever we go through, to have a space where we share our joys and concerns in a spiritual manner is a gift. Whatever we believe; wherever we can find it, bless'd be the tie that binds.

Chapter 34

When Morning Gilds The Sky

Text: Anonymous, *Katholisches Gesangbuch*, 1828
Translated by Edward Caswell, 1854
Music: Joseph Barnaby, *Hymns Ancient and Modern*, 1868

I think, perhaps, this hymn gets the prize for the best title. What a beautiful image! I'm sure that we can all visualize a spectacular sunrise filling the sky with golden beauty. It is my great fortune to be sitting in a sun-filled room as I write this, with the fresh spring air coming through windows that have finally been opened after a long winter.

The words for the hymn originate in a German text from the mid 1700s, and were translated into English in 1854. It was set to this tune in 1868 by Joseph Barnby, and was sung for the first time in St. Paul's Cathedral in London that year. If you've been in that space, one can easily imagine the combined beauty of the song with the architecture – it must have been a lovely experience!

This is quite simply a song of praise and gratitude. It is an exquisite collection of statements expressing that in beauty, in pain, in sadness, in darkness and in light, praise is given. There were, reportedly, 28 verses in the original hymn. I suppose that kind of length makes sense if we're trying to imagine every scenario life offers; every state of being that we can rise up from and fill our minds and hearts with praise.

When morning gilds the skies,
My heart awaking cries:
May Jesus Christ be praised!
Alike at work and prayer,
On him I cast my care.
May Jesus Christ be praised!

Does sadness fill my mind?
A solace here I find,
May Jesus Christ be praised!
Or fades my earthly bliss?
My comfort still is this,
May Jesus Christ be praised!

The night becomes as day
When from the heart we say:
May Jesus Christ be praised!
In heaven's eternal bliss
The loveliest strain is this:
May Jesus Christ be praised!

I hadn't heard this one in a while, and am so glad it was suggested to me. I can understand how it could be a favourite for many people. It has beautiful words and a beautiful tune. It has a beautiful message. Life has much in it, good and bad, but beauty prevails. It might be the beauty of the Divine or the beauty of faith. Or it might be a beauty yet to come. Maybe for you it's the beauty found in nature, or poetry, art, literature, or music. We all have the opportunity to find something that anchors us; something we can return to despite our earthly circumstances; something that becomes our eternal song, our song of praise; something that allows us to see the possibility of gilded skies.

Be this, while life is mine,
My canticle divine:
May Jesus Christ be praised!
Be this the eternal song,
Through all the ages long:
May Jesus Christ be praised!

Chapter 35

Joyful, Joyful, We Adore Thee

Text: Henry van Dyke, 1907
Music: Ludwig van Beethoven, 1823

> *Joyful, joyful, we adore Thee,*
> *God of glory, Lord of love;*
> *Hearts unfold like flowers before thee,*
> *praising thee their sun above.*
> *Melt the clouds of sin and sadness;*
> *drive the dark of doubt away.*
> *Giver of immortal gladness,*
> *fill us with the light of day!*

This song is widely known as the *Hymn to Joy*. It is probably the most popular hymn tune I've tackled this year, a tune that even my youngest piano students are familiar with and are happy to learn how to play. It is also a tune that routinely shows up in movies and commercials, and it is a hymn often sung, and part of a symphony regularly performed. We have Beethoven to thank for his exuberant *Ode to Joy* (1823) and Henry van Dyke for the poetry (1907) that together express this joy and allow us to participate in its singing.

This hymn celebrates sheer joy. It celebrates nature, love, friendship, and the ability of music to lift us above all we encounter. It is a song of life — a song for living the lives we are given. So I chose to place it on Mother's Day. What better way to celebrate our mothers than to live our lives fully? For the women who birthed us, for those who chose us, for those who raised us, for those who cared for us from afar, for those who took on the role of mentor and loved us. Their work, their tears, their struggles, their determination, their failings, their successes have all prepared us for our lives. They are a reflection of the creative power that fills our world.

> *All Thy works with joy surround thee,*
> *earth and heaven reflect Thy rays,*
> *Stars and angels sing around thee,*
> *center of unbroken praise.*
> *Field and forest, vale and mountain,*
> *blooming meadow, flashing sea,*
> *Chanting bird and flowing fountain*
> *call us to rejoice in Thee.*

Mothers do not always succeed, and for some, mothers have brought more pain than joy. But choosing to live joyfully while working through these tensions may allow us the space to forgive. Joy provides a window into a kind of love that can see beyond our failings and our mistakes.

Thou art giving and forgiving,
ever blessing, ever blessed,
Wellspring of the joy of living,
ocean depth of happy rest!
Thou our Father, Christ our Brother,
all who live in love are thine.
Teach us how to love each other,
lift us to the joy divine.

This is a hymn that we sing together — as children and as mothers. I suppose that we are all capable of participating in the act of mothering at some point in our lives, of providing what is needed for growth. I am once again thankful that music can remind me of this. I am hopeful that I will always choose to sing joyfully. But if I cannot, I hope I will still hear the happy chorus that is filled with mothers, sons and daughters, and be reassured that joy exists.

Mortals, join the happy chorus,
which the morning stars began;
Love divine is reigning o'er us,
leading us with mercy's hand.
Ever singing, march we onward,
victors in the midst of strife,
Joyful music lifts us sunward in
the triumph song of life.

Chapter 36

Jesus Loves Me

Text: Anna B. Warner, 1859
Music: William B. Bradbury, *The Golden Shower*, 1862

Children's songs are so familiar. They bring to us so many memories. I'm sure that most people who pick up this book will know this one, and perhaps they will have sung it as a child and probably can sing it from memory still. It may be the most well-known Sunday School song out there.

Having listened to our congregation sing it during a children's feature, it was clear to me that all the kids, young and old, knew the words and could sing along. So why is this one so enduring?

The origin of the text is interesting. It was actually a poem penned by Anna Bartlett Warner in 1860, to be used in a novel written by her sister, Susan Warner. The words were meant to comfort a dying child in the story. The original poem is full of comforting thoughts surrounding the strength of Jesus in contrast to the child's weakness and the assurance of being carried to heaven when death arrives. Comforting, perhaps, but also pretty bleak and very sad.

Jesus loves me—this I know,
For the Bible tells me so;
Little ones to him belong,
They are weak, but he is strong.

Jesus loves me—loves me still,
Though I'm very weak and ill;
From his shining throne on high,
Comes to watch me where I lie.

Jesus loves me—he will stay,
Close beside me all the way.
Then his little child will take,
Up to heaven for his dear sake.

I suppose that we all need something to carry us through the most difficult of moments. This hymn started its life as a means to do that. What could be more difficult than the death of a child? Surely, we all look for ways to provide comfort in these moments, and to give hope in situations that seem completely hopeless. I think the simplicity of this song and its sentiment of assurance that someone loves us enough to carry us through something horrific, is what makes it endure. It's a child's understanding of how to cope. Someone loves me, I'll be okay.

I appreciate that this is probably not a complete answer to many of our challenges. But there is something in the innocence of this belief that we can learn from both as givers and receivers of unconditional love. This kind of love doesn't solve our problems or eliminate suffering. But it does make things just a little more bearable. To face life's challenges without it seems so lonely and sad; almost inconceivable to those of us fortunate enough to have found a loving foundation to stand on. My hope is that we all find this kind of assurance and care, be it spiritual or earthly. My hope is also that we share this kind of assurance and care – through our lives, our actions, and our voices.

Chapter 37

Breathe One Me, Breath Of God

Text: Edwin Hatch, *Between Doubt and Prayer*, 1878
Music: Robert Jackson, *Fifty Sacred Leaflets*, 1888

Pentecost Sunday. As I looked into the history and meaning of this day, I found out that the word *Pentecost* comes from the Greek *Shavuot*, the feast commemorating the giving of the Law of Sinai, celebrated in Judaism. As is common with many feast days, it was later "borrowed" to mark the day that the Holy Spirit descended on the Apostles and other followers of Jesus.

The concept of the Holy Spirit is interesting to me. It comes up in a number of different religions; Christianity, Judaism, Islam, and Baha'i, to name a few. There are slightly different interpretations of what this spirit is, but the common link is that it is a conduit of God's wisdom. That is powerful and scary all at the same time. It is powerful because the possibility of receiving some Divine wisdom is extraordinary. It is scary because we are human, and separating our own views, ideas, and words from something greater than us, is very challenging.

The words of this hymn reflect the kind of humility required to find that wisdom, and they show the need to receive the breath of wisdom in order to access the depth of its knowledge.

Breathe on me, Breath of God,
fill me with life anew,
that I may love what thou dost love,
and do what thou wouldst do.

Breathe on me, Breath of God,
until my heart is pure,
until with thee I will one will,
to do and to endure.

Breathe on me, Breath of God,
till I am wholly thine,
till all this earthly part of me
glows with thy fire divine.

These words were written by Edwin Hatch in 1878. He was a well-educated man who taught the Classics and early Church History at Oxford. Yet these are fairly simple words. He seemed to understand the profound need for us to be humble and disciplined as we seek unity with God. It seems to me that humility is rare in most of our religious circles these days. There is much posturing and the need to be right and an impulse to speak as if our own ideas, interpretations, and traditions are, in fact, the wisdom of God. As a result, there is also much division, much conflict, and much pain.

As I continued to look into this idea of wisdom, the word *Sophia* kept coming up. This is probably a lesser known concept than the basic Pentecost story, but it was familiar to me. *Sophia* is the Greek word for wisdom and in some traditions, represents the feminine aspect of God. It is said that it is Sophia, or *Hagia Sophia* (holy wisdom) who circulates through and binds together the community. This is appealing to me. I like the idea that the Holy Spirit – Wisdom – can unify us. It is challenging, yes, because finding and receiving this spirit requires, perhaps, more humility than most of us can claim. But, on the Feast of Pentecost that is often called the birth of the Church, what a great way to consider this gift. May the Spirit of Wisdom unite you with whomever your community is. May it guide you and provide a space of peace.

Chapter 38

I Know Not Why God's Wondrous Grace

Text: Daniel W. Whittle, *Gospel Hymns, No. 4*, 1883
Music: James McGranaham, *Gospel Hymns, No. 4*, 1883

When this hymn was suggested to me by a friend, I hadn't thought of it in many years. I can't recall singing it recently, but it sure reminded me of my childhood. I'm not sure why it is connected to my childhood memories, but perhaps we sang it often at the church my family attended at the time. It's very familiar and I like it, in a sentimental way.

The words were written by Daniel Whittle around 1883. He was influenced by Dwight L. Moody to become an evangelist and travelled throughout the United States and Great Britain preaching and being accompanied by popular gospel singers of the time, including Philip Bliss and James McGranahan, who wrote the music.

I know not why God's wondrous grace
To me He hath made known,
Nor why, with mercy, Christ in love
Redeemed me for His own.

Refrain: But I know Whom I have believed,
And am persuaded that He is able
To keep that which I've committed
Unto Him against that day.

I know not how this saving faith
To me He did impart,
Nor how believing in His Word
Wrought peace within my heart.

I know not how the Spirit moves,
Convincing us of sin,
Revealing Jesus through the Word,
Creating faith in Him.

I know not when my Lord may come,
At night or noonday fair,
Nor if I'll walk the vale with Him,
Or meet Him in the air.

This is a hymn of contrasts. The verses describe everything that we cannot know. For example, we cannot understand God's grace, and we cannot comprehend God's Spirit, and we don't really understand why faith brings us peace, and we don't know what the future holds. And yet, the refrain professes a confidence in a belief that carries us – and everything we struggle with – to the end of earthly life. I suppose this is at the crux of what faith is: understanding that we simply do not have all the answers, but believing in something anyway. Regardless of the details of what we don't really understand or what we believe, this is difficult. Sometimes trusting that there is something that can carry the weight we bear in this life seems impossible.

I guess that I kind of like this contrast. I like that this hymn acknowledges the struggle. In an era obsessed with sound bites that claim to be absolutes and complete philosophies reduced to a sentence or less, I'm fine with not knowing. I don't really need all the answers. Sometimes it's enough to know that the foundation I've chosen, built, and stand on, will survive the challenges and questions; the debates and arguments; and even the unknown. Sometimes survival includes some improvements. Sometimes it means expansion and new growth. Sometimes it means making necessary reductions. Whatever foundation you choose for your life, build it well and make it strong. Use strong materials, know what they are, and then let them guide and support you through this unknowable life.

Chapter 39

All Creatures Of Our God And King

Text: Francis of Assisi, 1255
Music: *Kirchengesangbuch, Cologne,* 1623

> *All creatures of our God and King,*
> *lift up your voice and with us sing,*
> *Alleluia! Alleluia!*
> *O brother sun with golden beam,*
> *O sister moon with silver gleam!*
> *O sing ye! O sing ye!*
> *Alleluia! Alleluia! Alleluia!*

I love this hymn. It is so joyful. If you take the time to consider all seven verses, it simply exhorts the whole planet to sing. What a great idea. Sun, moon, wind, air, clouds, water, fire and light. Sorrow, pain, tender hearts, and death. Lifting voices; singing together.

We can thank Saint Francis of Assisi for these exuberant words. He wrote them around 1225, and they are considered to be one of the oldest hymn texts still in use. Francis of Assisi was a radical in his time. He abandoned luxury at a time of extreme decadence within the church and encouraged a life of poverty and peace. It is no surprise, reading these words, that he has also become the patron saint of ecologists. Clearly, he loved and valued creation.

> *Dear mother earth, who day by day*
> *unfoldest blessings on our way,*
> *Alleluia! Alleluia!*
> *The flowers and fruits that in thee grow,*
> *let them God's glory also show!*
> *O sing ye! O sing ye!*
> *Alleluia! Alleluia! Alleluia!*

So sing. Look around and see the world in its beauty. Treasure it – this place where we live, breathe, and die. This place we share. This place worth singing about. *Sing!* And let it prompt a life worthy of the song.

Chapter 40

Heilig, Heilig, Heilig

Text: Johann Philipp Neuman, c. 1826
Music: Franz Schubert, *Gesänger zur Feier des heilgen Opfer der Messe*, 1826

Heilig, heilig, heilig, heilig ist derr Herr!
Heilig, heilig, heilig, heilig ist nur Er!
Holy, holy, holy, holy is the Lord!
Holy, holy, holy, holy God alone!

It was a beautiful spring day as I began to ponder this hymn. I don't know why I chose to place it that week, but as I listened to the breeze rustling through the leaves outside my window, I think maybe it was meant to remind me of the value of holiness. As I looked for a definition of the word holy, I found that it is sort of difficult to pin down. It can mean sacred and worthy of devotion; it can mean spiritual or religious. It can be about spaces, behaviours, people, and the Divine. It's a little bit mysterious – and it is something I suspect we don't contemplate very often in our modern world.

This hymn comes from Schubert's *Deutsche Messe* (German Mass; 1827). It is the *Sanctus* portion of the mass, which is a prayer of thanks to God – sung with the angels, who are said to sing

"Holy, Holy, Holy" unceasingly. Apparently, this element of the liturgy is one of the oldest we have evidence of, dating back to St. Clement of Rome who died around the year 104. So the church has been honouring this holiness with song for almost two thousand years, probably longer. Interesting.

Er, der nie begonen, er, der immer war,
ewig ist und waltet, sein wird immerdar.
He who never began, He who always was,
He who eternally is and reigns, and will always be.

There is something peaceful about this music. The words are simple. The description of God is powerful. God is not created. No matter how we try to craft the Divine in our image, that simply isn't the nature of this holiness. And I think we do that often. It seems like we desperately want to understand this thing that is beyond us. We want a God that makes sense. We want a God to back our ideas and justify our actions. We want a God that looks like us. But the Divine will not be diminished to fit into our ideas and spaces.

In a world where everything has been reduced to the easily grasped and the familiar, finding holiness becomes our challenge. This is because we need mystery, and we need awe. Wonder reminds us of our smallness in the universe while it gives us an understanding of our worth. And we are worthy of holiness.

Like the sound of the breeze in the trees, there is a peaceful mystery to the holy. Listen.

Chapter 41

Praise, My Soul, The King Of Heaven

Text: Ps. 103, Henry F. Lyte, *Spirit of the Psalms*, 1834
Music: John Goss, *The Supplement Hymn & Tune Book,* 1869

This hymn is quite simply a song of praise. Praise. I had to give that some thought. It's a word used often in church settings. It's a word that describes a kind of gift we can bestow upon someone or something we really and truly admire. Something we endorse. Something we find to be great.

In this case, the poet Henry Francis Lyte (1793-1847) was trying to capture the spirit of Psalm 103 in song; a spirit of a whole hearted praise of God.

> *Praise, my soul, the King of Heaven;*
> *To His feet thy tribute bring.*
> *Ransomed, healed, restored, forgiven,*
> *Who like me His praise should sing?*
> *Alleluia! Alleluia!*
> *Praise the everlasting King.*
>
> *Praise Him for His grace and favour*
> *To all people in distress.*
> *Praise Him still the same as ever,*
> *Slow to chide, and swift to bless.*

Alleluia! Alleluia!
Glorious in His faithfulness.

These words were particularly suitable when we were celebrating Fathers' Day during the week I originally wrote this. As I reflected, I found within the third verse a description of the care and gentle nature a father should exhibit. God as father can sometimes overwhelm – both as a standard to live up to and as a singularly overused metaphor. But in this case, it is a beautiful reminder of the traits that are worthy of praise. Being fatherlike means providing gentle, knowing care.

Fatherlike He tends and spares us;
Well our feeble frame He knows.
In His hands He gently bears us,
Rescues us from all our foes.
Alleluia! Alleluia!
Widely yet His mercy flows.

As I thought more about these words, it occurred to me that the characteristics inspiring praise might well be a guide for all of us. Grace and favour towards those in distress, slow to chide, swift to bless, tending and gently bearing. I think these are indeed characteristics worthy of praise, although I sometimes wonder if they are the characteristics that we actually value. It seems that words like successful, popular, accomplished and powerful engender more praise in our culture. Yet, for hundreds of years, images of the Divine have been crafted through words, music, and art while inspiring praise of tenderness, joy, care, and grace. Perhaps we should pay heed to this history, praise that which is worthy, and live lives that are worthy of praise.

> *Angels, help us to adore Him;*
> *Ye behold Him face to face;*
> *Sun and moon, bow down before Him,*
> *Dwellers all in time and space.*
> *Alleluia! Alleluia!*
> *Praise with us the God of grace.*

Chapter 42

In The Rifted Rock I'm Resting

Text: Mary Dagworthy James, *The Chautauqua Collection*, 1875
Music: W. Warren Bentley, *The Chautauqua Collection*, 1875

A number of years ago I arranged this hymn as a gift for my mother-in-law's birthday. When it was suggested for my list of hymns this year, I debated whether I should re-arrange it or just use the one I had already done. It felt strange to change something I had given as a gift, so this was the lone repeat for my year of song! It also happened to be her birthday that week, so again I give this gift.

This is a hymn that, in my Mennonite heritage, is often associated with the long journey of those who left Ukraine in the early 1900s and came to Canada and the United States. It is a story of hardship, persecution, escape, and arrival in a new land with new challenges and opportunities. It is a history steeped in the idea that faith carries one through difficult times, and this hymn's words reflect this.

In the rifted rock I'm resting,
Safely sheltered I abide;
There no foes nor storms molest me,
While within the cleft I hide.

Refrain:

Now I'm resting, sweetly resting,
In the cleft once made for me;
Jesus, blessed Rock of Ages,
I will hide myself in Thee.

Long pursued by sin and Satan,
Weary, sad, I longed for rest;
Then I found this heav'nly shelter
Opened in my Savior's breast.

Peace which passeth understanding,
Joy the world can never give,
Now in Jesus I am finding,
In His smiles of love I live.

In the rifted rock I'll hide me,
Till the storms of life are past;
All secure in this blest refuge,
Heeding not the fiercest blast.

The friend who suggested this hymn mentioned that her daughters were learning to play this hymn for their dying grandfather's funeral. I found that quite moving. For them, it reflects their ancestral history, their faith story, a gift of music to comfort those who remain and an understanding of the peaceful rest their loved one would find after his passing. How beautiful. How peace-filled.

This is a song that speaks of a longing for peace. While recognizing the many challenges of life and the storms and the fierce blasts, it is a plea for rest. I suppose we all need a place to find rest. We live turbulent lives and there is little protection from these storms and blasts. Finding a place that keeps us safe is something that we all seek. Using our gifts to give a little bit of that shelter to those in our lives is a good and valuable occupation. I imagine my ancestors singing this song and suspect they were doing just that. I ponder two girls playing beautiful music in memory of their grandfather and think they are doing it as well. Give someone a space for rest – with song, deed, and care. Life's storms are cold, but our gifts can warm, shelter, and protect.

Chapter 43

Be Still My Soul

Text: Katharina A. von Schlegel, *Neue Sammlung Geistlicher Lieder*, 1752
Music: Jean Sibelius, *Finlandia*, 1899

> *Be still, my soul: the Lord is on thy side.*
> *Bear patiently the cross of grief or pain.*
> *Leave to thy God to order and provide;*
> *In every change, He faithful will remain.*
> *Be still, my soul: thy best, thy heav'nly Friend*
> *Through thorny ways leads to a joyful end.*

As I think about the many hymns I've looked at, there are a few common themes that come up again and again. One of these themes is pain and the desire to find a peace that can bear it. Over and over, I've read words that must have emerged from great challenges, fears, disappointments and deep grief. Over and over the authors of these words have stressed that there is something greater than the pain. That there is hope.

> *Be still, my soul: the hour is hast'ning on*
> *When we shall be forever with the Lord.*
> *When disappointment, grief, and fear are gone,*

Sorrow forgot,
love's purest joys restored.
Be still, my soul:
when change and tears are past
All safe and blessed we shall meet at last.

This hymn speaks to this theme. It came to my list via someone who admitted that many hymns stirred feelings of awe and occasional tears. He shared that his feelings varied when hearing the same hymn in different contexts and occasions. I found that interesting, particularly with this tune, written by Jean Sibelius in 1899/1900 for a symphonic poem, the theme of which became a song (*Finlandia*) that has been used like a national anthem in Finland and a hymn in many, many churches. It is a beautiful melody that can evoke different emotions depending on the context.

These particular words predate the tune by many years, written originally in German by Katherine von Schlegel in 1725, and translated into English by British poet Jane Borthwick in 1855. What a history it is, crossing nations, languages, and musical forms. For me, therein lies one of the great beauties of hymnody. It spans so much. It gives glimpses into both the challenges and the inspirations searched for and found by those who wrote the words and the music.

So we have difficult themes and we have hopeful responses, and we discover that we all have and need both, and that it's been this way forever. Sometimes we are lifted up. Sometimes we are not. But we are not alone. The experiences of pain and hope are shared by us all — now, in the past, and in the future. Despite our differences, we are all just souls in search of stillness. There is comfort in that knowledge. There is joy, and there is peace.

> ***Be still, my soul: the Sun of life divine***
> ***Through passing clouds***
> ***shall but more brightly shine.***

Chapter 44

Come, Let Us All Unite To Sing

Text: Anonymous, *Millennial Praises*, 1812
Music: Edmund S. Lorenz, *Notes of Triumph: for the Sunday School*, 1886

> *Come, let us all unite to sing: God is love!*
> *Let Heav'n and earth their praises bring,*
> *God is love! Let every soul from sin awake,*
> *Let every heart sweet music make,*
> *And sing with us for Jesus' sake: God is love!*

A hymn full of cheer. A hymn that asks everyone to join in and sing. Sing because God is love. I suppose that's as good a reason to sing as any, the idea that this Divine being is love. It's kind of a grand concept. Not simply that God loves us or that we love God, but that God *is* love.

I must admit that love is another one of our commonly used words that is actually quite difficult to define. We understand it as a feeling of affection, attraction, or devotion and a means of expression. It is something that compels us to act in a particular way, and something that can shape our views, our actions, and our decisions. But, for something or someone to be love, seems beyond our usual definitions.

How happy is our portion here, God is love!
His promises our spirits cheer, God is love!
He is our sun and shield by day,
Our help, our hope, our strength and stay;
He will be with us all the way; God is love!

The words of this hymn first appeared in 1812 in an American songbook called *Millennial Praises*. It is unknown who wrote them, although they are sometimes attributed to Howard Kingsbury (which is unlikely, as he was only born in 1842!). It's interesting to me that they are so pleasant and filled with images of sweet music, happiness, sunshine, hope, and strength. Sing praises and all will be well. While I will be the first to suggest that music can uplift, and that the act of praise, in whatever form or tradition you choose to practice, may also boost the spirit, life doesn't magically become all we desire just because we're singing praises.

So I struggle with these kinds of words. If we can't praise, do we become sad? If we are struggling, hopeless, depressed, sick, or weak then are we unable to praise? Have we failed? I don't think so. I think we have just been unable to define love very well. Love encompasses us completely. Not just the happy bits, not just what looks or feels good. To me, these cheerful words are only part of the story. I'm happy to unite to sing, but love is about more than sunshine and so I also need us to sing in and about the rain.

Unite to sing whatever words or tune you know. There is much to be found in the unity of singing together. But if you find yourself in a moment where you have no song, simply listen – the rest of us will sing. And we will fill our voices with whatever love we have.

God is love! God is love!
Come let us all unite to sing that God is love.

Chapter 45

Amazing Grace

Text: John Newton, *Olnet Hymns*, 1779
Music: American Folk Melody, *Virginia Harmony*, 1831

It's hard to imagine a year of reflections on our favourite hymns without *Amazing Grace* making an appearance. It is a hymn that is not only common in most Christian churches, but it also makes regular appearances in popular culture and political contexts. It is not simply a familiar hymn, but in fact some have argued that it is the most well-known song in the English-speaking world.

The story of this hymn is quite famous. Movies have been made about it, books and articles have been written, and there was even a Broadway show telling the tale. The words were written by John Newton following his conversion experience. This spiritual event took place during a violent storm while at sea as a slave trader in 1748. Following the experience, he continued in the slave trade until around 1755 when he began studying theology and eventually became an ordained minister in the Church of England. The words have been associated with more than 20 melodies, but the one we are familiar with emerged in 1831.

Amazing grace how sweet the sound
that saved a wretch like me!
I once was lost but now am found,
was blind but now I see.
'Twas grace that taught my heart to fear,
and grace my fears relieved;
how precious did that grace appear
the hour I first believed!

Through many dangers, toils, and snares
I have already come;
'tis grace hath brought me safe thus far,
and grace will lead me home.

When we've been there ten thousand years,
bright shining as the sun,
we've no less days to sing God's praise
than when we'd first begun.

Few of us will have the experience of receiving grace for something as horrific as being a slave trader. But grace need not be applied only to the grandest of transgressions. Grace is about mercy, kindness, pardon, forgiveness, and acceptance. Grace is a treasured gift we can receive, be it Divine or otherwise. But as I ponder this hymn, I wonder if its power lies more in our ability to provide it to those in our lives and to ourselves. We are easily hurt and disappointed by a whole variety of acts, comments, and failures. We are critical of others and ourselves. We live in a world where the ability to comment on almost anything anybody says or does is extremely easy. We have moments of compassion and encouragement, but I'm not sure we really know how to extend grace. This is especially because extending grace doesn't really require the offender to change or be better. Grace just forgives, and it is unmerited. This is a huge challenge for us. Would we forgive a slave trader who carried on for seven more years? I doubt it.

I will struggle with this concept for a while yet, but I can see the potential in it. When I receive grace, I am so much closer to where I should be – whether I choose to change or not. Giving this kind of forgiveness and care is a selfless act that may never see any return. And yet, using one's life to open this kind of door for others is valuable. Open doors offer so much more than those that are closed – even if no one ever walks through them, they can see the view.

Chapter 46
Lead Me, Lord

Text: Based on Psalm 5:8
Music: Samuel Wesley, 1861

This hymn comes to us from a friend who said that he often found himself praying it when he needed guidance or direction. I thought that was a beautiful way to think of a hymn – as a prayer. I know that many hymns are just that, but this is a tiny gem that asks very simply for a clear view of where to go and how to find safety.

> *Lead me, Lord, lead me in thy righteousness,*
> *make thy way plain before my face.*
> *For it is thou, Lord, thou, Lord only,*
> *that makest me dwell in safety.*

I couldn't find a great deal of information about this hymn but it was written in 1861 by Samuel Sebastian Wesley, the grandson of the more famous hymn writer Charles Wesley. At the time it was popular to write what were known as verse anthems. In combination with unison and choral parts, these multi-sectional pieces were designed to show off the talents of the various soloists within a church choir. *Lead Me Lord* is an excerpt from one of these longer anthems called *Praise the Lord, O My Soul.*

I think that the sentiment of these words is quite powerful. The idea that walking in righteousness clarifies our path and leads to safety is something for us to consider. I appreciate that the language used here carries a bit of baggage for some of us – righteousness sounds close to self-righteousness and implies a very specific way of understanding the world. But when I look at what righteousness actually means – justice, decency, honesty – I find myself thinking that this is, indeed, a way to clarify the path I want to be on. Making decisions about how I want to live based on the notion of justice also leads me on a very specific path, and the safety found on that path is beyond my own. Justice requires safety for all. For me, to dwell in safety requires a broader understanding than simply a personal space for myself and those closest to me. The safety of the few is thin, and it is unjust.

So as I pray this hymn, my hope is that I will see clearly the path of real righteousness and that I will have the courage to walk that path. A path that is paved with justice and provides safety for all. This is where I wish to dwell.

Chapter 47

Holy, Holy, Holy

Text: Reginald Heber, *A Selection of Psalms and Hymns*, 1826
Music: John B. Dykes, *Hymns Ancient and Modern*, 1861

> *Holy, Holy, Holy! Lord God Almighty!*
> *Early in the morning*
> *our song shall rise to Thee;*
> *Holy, Holy, Holy! Merciful and Mighty!*
> *God in three persons, blessed trinity!*

This is another very familiar hymn – one that I know extremely well and could almost sing from memory. It was written by Reginald Heber in 1826 for Trinity Sunday, the day that has traditionally celebrated the doctrine of the Holy Trinity established by the Council of Nicaea in 325. The tune, written by John B. Dykes in 1861, named *Nicaea*, also commemorates this significant event.

Well, that's the history. And, no, it isn't Trinity Sunday (that would be the first Sunday following Pentecost, sometime in the spring). This one came to my list with a story that had nothing to do with its history; a story unrelated to the meaning of its words. This story is about a five-year-old child struggling in new surroundings and being encouraged by this hymn. Attending a small church that had a time for song requests at the end of their service, this child would often ask to sing this hymn, much to the amusement of the adults! But they would sing it enthusiastically and the memory of this community support stayed with my friend into adulthood. This was partly because they indulged him and partly because it created an image of a united group walking through life together.

It's interesting to me how powerful our communities can be; how much they can carry us through our lives; how much they shape the way we interact with our world. This story once again reminds me that we have no idea what the impact of listening to, and really hearing, a small voice will be. There are always consequences to how we respond to voices around us. We can encourage, discourage, challenge, inspire, deflate, and support. We can educate and be educated. We can tear down or we can build up. Sometimes it's difficult to figure out which response is the positive one, but the lesson I take from this child's experience is that being heard is the starting point.

Finding a community that encourages our voices is truly a gift. Being a community that listens, is both a challenge and a privilege. So early in the morning when our songs are rising, I hope there is space to hear all who wish to sing.

*Holy, Holy, Holy! Lord God Almighty!
All Thy works shall praise thy name in
earth and sky and sea;
Holy, Holy, Holy! Merciful and Mighty!
God in Three Persons, blessed Trinity!*

Chapter 48

He Leadeth Me

Text: Joseph H. Gilmore, *Watchman & Reflector*, 1862
Music: William B. Bradbury, *The Golden Censer*, 1864

Imagine it is the middle of a war and you read the Twenty-Third Psalm. Arriving at the words "He leadeth me," you are unable to continue. The very idea of being led through extreme difficulty stops you in your tracks. This is the story of Joseph H. Gilmore who wrote the words to this hymn in 1862 during the American Civil War. There is something very powerful about his experience of finding comfort in this sentiment that the very thing he chose to put his faith in was guiding him through what must have been very dark days.

> *He leadeth me, O blessed thought!*
> *O words with heav'nly comfort fraught!*
> *Whate'er I do, where'er I be*
> *Still 'tis God's hand that leadeth me.*
>
> *Sometimes mid scenes of deepest gloom,*
> *Sometimes where Eden's bowers bloom,*
> *By waters still, over troubled sea,*
> *Still 'tis His hand that leadeth me.*

What struck me as I read this story was that, in what are purported to be Gilmore's own words, "it makes no difference how we are led, or whither we are led, so long as we are sure God is leading us." It was his faith and belief that were important, not the details of his life or the circumstances in which he found himself. For me, this is a perspective that is often lost. We live in a time when results are the primary motivation for everything, especially when they lead to or show off success, wealth, fame, and recognition. We wish to be led in the *right* direction – not just led. Our beliefs and values often seem to be constructed to fit the reward, be it material or spiritual. And yet, look around. The diversity in the results people experience is overwhelming. By our popular measures of success, it would seem that very few are following a good leader. So few people achieve the dream we are presented with; the ideal life is hard to attain.

These words are about faith and conviction. They are about the conscious act of allowing whatever it is that we believe to guide us. Our obsession with results makes this seem almost countercultural. We want to win, we want to achieve change, we want to accomplish things, and we want to succeed. All of these goals can be good, but when we are driven solely by these things life is fast and empty. Standing on the foundation of what you believe and what you truly value, provides a better view – of the good and of the bad. Taking in that view is inherently worthwhile, providing boundless opportunities for ourselves and those around us, for our world and our communities. So I encourage you to really look toward whatever leads you. If you have chosen wisely, it will carry you wherever you need to go.

He leadeth me, He leadeth me,
By His own hand He leadeth me;
His faithful follower I would be,
For by His hand He leadeth me.

Chapter 49

My Life Flows On

Text and Music: Robert S. Lowry, *Bright Jewels for Sunday School*, 1869

> *My life flows on in endless song;*
> *above earth's lamentation,*
> *I catch the sweet, though far-off hymn*
> *that hails a new creation.*

When I started my year of song, I received a number of personal comments from those who made suggestions of hymns for me to consider. This is the last story that I have to share from that list. I have placed this beautiful hymn near the end of my year because it contains the line, "how can I keep from singing?" If there is one thing that drove me to do this project, that is probably it. There is something about all that life contains that requires me to sing, and to sing in many tunes, and with many words, and many emotions.

> *Through all the tumult and the strife,*
> *I hear that music ringing.*
> *It finds an echo in my soul.*
> *How can I keep from singing?*

The gift of this hymn, written in the mid 1800s by Robert Lowry, came from a fellow pianist who started out by saying that while it is a lovely song, she has often been annoyed by its lack of a time signature. However, she also acknowledged that somehow a beautiful character emerges from this very thing. There's an uncertainty in the rhythm that, despite our desire for a regular beat, presents us with something both soothing and meaningful. It is a little like finding a song to sing in spite of the uncertainties of life.

It is dear to me that this friend also shared that her mother had requested that this be sung at her funeral. Knowing this has made it difficult for her to sing those famous, repeated words, "how can I keep from singing?" because the reality of that day seemed to creep closer. But she loves the hymn anyway, and it remains a treasure for her. I am once again struck by how words and music carry, through time, our common experiences, all while providing comfort and space to let our emotions flow.

What though my joys and comforts die?
I know my Savior liveth.
What though the darkness gather round?
Songs in the night he giveth.

Whenever I listen to this hymn and sing it, I will be reminded of this shared story. The combination of beauty, annoyance, recognition, sorrow, as well as comfort make for mixed emotions. So many of these hymns speak of the range of our experiences while recognizing that life just isn't simple. But sometimes they also state the really simple ideas that can provide us with so much more than we expect. This one is like that. It reminds us that we all have a voice and were made to sing. We have a built in instrument that has no equal, and whether it is our inner or outer voice, it is one that can sooth, weep, uplift, and inspire. I am unendingly grateful for the gift of singing – whether it's done out loud or silently, in community or alone. Sing.

> *No storm can shake my inmost calm*
> *while to that Rock I'm clinging.*
> *Since Christ is Lord of heaven and earth,*
> *how can I keep from singing?*

Chapter 50

Abide With Me

Text: Henry F. Lyte, 1847
Music: William H. Monk, *Hymns Ancient and Modern*, 1861

As I neared the end of my year of song, I felt it fitting to include this beautiful hymn. This is one that is usually reserved for funerals, but it also speaks to our many endings, and it speaks to our fears about what the future holds.

> *Abide with me; fast falls the eventide;*
> *The darkness deepens; Lord with me abide.*
> *When other helpers fail, and comforts flee,*
> *Help of the helpless, O abide with me.*

The story goes that these words were written in 1847 by Henry F. Lyte as he lay dying from tuberculosis. Although, I also read that he was haunted by the phrase "abide with me" that had been repeatedly muttered by a friend who was dying. Either way, there is a sense of desperation in these words; a sense of urgent need when passing into the unknown – in this life or the next.

This is a hymn that has offered comfort to many. When William Monk wrote the familiar tune in 1861, he apparently did so to help his wife get through a difficult time. And there are many other stories of its use. Everything from being played on the deck of the *Titanic* as it sunk to being sung in the trenches of World War I. It was used as a theme in a prelude by Ralph Vaughan Williams and recorded by Thelonious Monk with his jazz septet. It is even said to have been a favourite of Mahatma Gandhi.

> *Swift to its close ebbs out life's little day;*
> *Earth's joys grow dim; its glories pass away;*
> *Change and decay in all around I see;*
> *O Thou who changest not, abide with me.*

What I take from all of this is that fear of the unknown is pretty common. There is much in life and death that we do not understand. Try as we might to find answers, there frequently aren't any. Often what we think will lie at the end of any path, is simply not there at all.

> *Thou on my head in early youth didst smile,*
> *And though rebellious and perverse meanwhile,*
> *Thou hast not left me, oft as I left Thee.*
> *On to the close, O Lord, abide with me.*

When endings arrive, we all need something to bear us onward into the unknown, and something that reassures us in the midst of uncertainty and sometimes in real fear. We need to feel cradled in care — or at least as though we don't walk alone. What comes next isn't always bad, but not knowing is frightening and difficult when faced alone. These words are not about finding answers or ignoring reality. They are about finding something that will be a companion along the path of the unknown. Something that will listen when the words "abide with me" are spoken; something to cradle that request and fill our view with peace.

I need Thy presence every passing hour.
What but Thy grace can foil
the tempter's power?
Who, like Thyself, my guide and stay can be?
Through cloud and sunshine, Lord,
abide with me.

Chapter 51

The Day Thou Gavest, Lord, Is Ended

Text: John Ellerton, *Church Hymns*, 1870/71
Music: Clement C. Scholefield, *Church Hymns with Tunes 4*, 1874

> *The day Thou gavest, Lord, is ended,*
> *The darkness falls at Thy behest;*
> *To Thee our morning hymns ascended,*
> *Thy praise shall sanctify our rest.*

I love the evening. The calm found in darkness. The night sky, stars, and the moon. Although I don't often have the luxury of doing so, there is nothing better than playing piano late into the night when it feels like the rest of the world is sleeping. There is something about filling that kind of silence with music that brings to mind a space far greater than the room I'm in. This hymn reminds me of that space; of the world out there that carries on when we sleep, and of the world that needs to be cared for whether we can see it or not.

We thank Thee that Thy church, unsleeping,
While earth rolls onward into light,
Through all the world her watch is keeping,
And rests not now by day or night.

The words to this hymn were written by John Ellerton in 1871, reportedly on his nightly walk to a teaching position he held. Not surprisingly to those of us who enjoy late night walks, it is easy to imagine how creativity can emerge from this profound activity. It is also easy to imagine that creativity *should* emerge when we come to the end of the day. The cycle of day to night and night to day is so much a part of us and this hymn reflects the idea that every end is also a beginning.

As o'er each continent and island
The dawn leads on another day,
The voice of prayer is never silent,
Nor dies the strain of praise away.

The sun that bids us rest is waking
Our brethren 'neath the western sky,
And hour by hour fresh lips are making
Thy wondrous doings heard on high.

So as I relish the evening, I need to consider what follows. All the possibilities that emerge from the end of one day and the beginning of the next. And the thing that flows between; the thing that holds us together as we pass from night to day and back. This is our treasure. Find it and let it share the calm space of the night, and the joy of the new day.

So be it, Lord; Thy throne shall never,
Like earth's proud empires, pass away:
Thy kingdom stands, and grows forever,
Till all Thy creatures own Thy sway.

Chapter 52

Praise God From Whom All Blessings Flow

Text: Thomas Ken, *A Manual of Prayers for the Use of Scholars in Winchester College*, 1695
Music: Louis Bourgeois, *Genevan Psalter*, 1551
Music: *Boston Handel and Haydn Society Collection*, 1830

We have come to the end of my year of song. So now I give you a doxology. The word doxology comes from two Greek words – *doxa*, which means 'glory' and *logia*, which means 'saying'. This combination means a short statement of praise usually added to the end of canticles, psalms and, fittingly for this situation, hymns.

This was an interesting year. When I began this project, I really didn't consider it to be anything more than a means to motivate myself to do music. It was a deadline, of sorts, that would force me to work at something I wasn't otherwise obligated to do – having no boss to please or paycheque to earn for my labours. Well, it did that, and then some.

I learned many things.

I have learned that people love hymns. They are old and some may find their words and their music outdated, but many of us love them anyway. Many of us are comforted by their familiarity; by the depth of their texts and by the history that has carried them to us. There are truths to be found whether we agree with every word or not. This is one of the great beauties of art – be it musical or poetic, visual or literary. There is more there than appears on the surface.

I have learned that it is possible to find beauty in places I had thought ugly. Some of these hymns were not my favourites. In asking others for their suggestions, I hadn't considered what I might receive! To be perfectly honest, I genuinely disliked some of these hymns when I started. I didn't like all the tunes and I definitely had serious challenges with many of the texts. But in the end, I am deeply grateful for having been given the task of finding meaning despite my personal tastes, beliefs and perspectives. What a valuable lesson.

I have learned that I am part of a community, one that is both easily and not easily defined, and one that has become a little larger throughout this project. It contains both friends and strangers; people with diverse beliefs. It has overwhelmed me with support. Time and again I have received incredibly kind words and sharing of personal experiences related to many of these hymns, as well as much encouragement regarding the musical arrangements and thoughts I've shared. Endless positivity. In a world where one often hesitates to read comments sections, I had exactly zero negative or critical responses to this project.

So beauty, community, and the shared appreciation of these hymns emerge as ever-present centerpieces on my table. They are a pretty good reward for the task, and a pretty good flow of blessings.

> *Praise God, from whom all blessings flow;*
> *Praise him, all creatures here below;*
> *Praise him above, ye heavenly host;*
> *Praise Father, Son, and Holy Ghost.*

Amen

Carla Klassen is a piano teacher, accompanist, professional chorister, and church musician. She has been singing her whole life and has spent the past number of years rediscovering traditional hymns as an arranger, having arranged for piano more than one hundred and fifty of these sacred songs. When she is not making music, she is an avid traveler, art lover, and collector of all sorts of treasures.

Pandora Press is an independent publisher focusing on scholarly and popular titles in Anabaptist Mennonite Studies and beyond.

For a catalogue of recent publications, details for submitting manuscripts, and contact information please see our website: www.pandorapress.com

www.ingramcontent.com/pod-product-compliance
Lightning Source LLC
Chambersburg PA
CBHW031317160426
43196CB00007B/572